"You're going to love Ka ~~beautiful devotional,~~ *Arise! ~~You are Called to Be a Woman of Influ~~ence*, first in a series of many to come. Katie and Philipa have given their lives as encouragers of women worldwide. They are able to get heart deep with the reader as they share testimonies of their own intimate struggles and triumphs. This devotional book would make a great gift for any woman who needs a little extra encouragement to rise up in her gifting and calling. Katie and Philipa have an incredible ability to communicate the extravagant heart of the Father and His powerful ability to work great and mighty works in and through women no matter who they are!"

—Candice and Brian Simmons,
The Passion Translation Project

"The impact of this collection of life's experiences, devotional directions, and nuggets of encouragement affected me like water to a thirsty desert floor."

—Jacqueline F. Keish,
Ph.D., Southlake, TX

"*Arise! You are Called to Be a Woman of Influence* brought me to a closer, more personal relationship with my Lord Jesus Christ. It reminded me of what He really sees in me and how I can live up to my full potential as a child of God. Each day I looked forward to reading the beautiful words of truth that I so desperately needed to hear. Katie and Philipa have a powerful message for all women, no matter their age or season of life. We must see ourselves as Christ sees us!

—Lindsay Salter,
Director of Illuminate Ministries, Bossier City, LA

"The *Arise! You are Called to Be a Woman of Influence* devotional is an inspiring, honest, deeply affirming, and hope-filled read. The authors have shared impacting insights gained from their own everyday life experiences. At times, painful experiences, whilst remaining transparent about their questions and doubts when faced with confronting issues. Reading this, I felt like I was sitting having a conversation with a much-loved friend who was encouraging me to 'lift my eyes towards heaven' and to walk in the true identity of influence and purpose bestowed on me as a daughter of the Most High God. Deeply loved and perfectly empowered! If you are wanting a daily dose of uplifting truth and encouragement, I would love to recommend this devotional."

—Catherine Hoekendijk, Senior Pastor,
Harmony Church, Christchurch, New Zealand

"Such a great reminder to women of all ages of our impact on the kingdom."

—Becky Cole,
Author of *Tell Someone*, Austin, TX

"A powerful reminder of God's love for us, *Arise! You are Called to Be a Woman of Influence* is great for women of all ages and stages. Reading this devotional fills me with God-given energy to more boldly pursue God's specific plan and purpose for my life, and serves as a reminder of how important our influence as a woman is to others."

—Paige Murphy,
President, Blue Ripple Investment Group, INC, Atlanta, GA

AMAZON REVIEWS:

"I love this book's message to women--we are loved, cherished, and made to be world changers! This book will encourage you to discover your purpose in Christ and how He made you to be an influencer."

—Amazon Customer 5 star review

"This is an incredible devotional for women to be encouraged, supported, and inspired. The pages are filled with the Word of God and deep meaning. I recommend this book to women of any age."

—KB, Friendswood, TX 5 star review

"Each day focuses on a different attribute of a woman (you-the reader) and inspires you to go out and BE all that you were created to be! You'll be blessed as you discover more about how you can use your influence to make an impact on those around you."

—Reading Mom, Amazon review 5 stars

ARISE!

ARISE!

YOU ARE CALLED TO BE A WOMAN OF INFLUENCE

KATIE WALKER
PHILIPA A. BOOYENS

CONTENTS

A great awakening is coming,
and it is coming through you.
Woman of Influence,
it is time for you to arise.

"Who is this one? Look at her now!
She arises out of her desert,
clinging to her beloved..."

—*Song of Songs 8:5, TPT*—

Acknowledgments

Jaco and Philipa A. Booyens: Your constant encouragement, support, and love push me to reach higher, and dream beyond my ability. Without your expertise, this project would not have been possible. I am blessed to call you family. Thank you. I love and appreciate you with all my heart.

The After Eden Team: You are the family that continues to blow on the burning fuse in my heart, helping me to passionately seek Christ with all my might. You've encouraged and supported me every step of the way. Much love to you all.

Jan Burns: My mom, who we call "Honey" in my home. I want to thank you with all my heart for being the greatest cheerleader to my every dream, a warrior intercessor, and my best friend. You know me the best and love me anyway. The best is yet to come. I love you.

My children: Riley, Jack, Presley, and Shea: May you continue to grow to love the Lord your God with all your heart and lean on Him with your all. May my ceiling be your floor. I love you forever.

Women of Insight: Thank you for contributing to the first edition of this book. You are loved and beyond beautiful. Your voice will always matter, and, without it, this book wouldn't be.

To my husband, Todd: When God gave me you, he gave me the best. Your unconditional love and support have given me the courage to step into so many new adventures. Your loyalty and support give me so much joy, and I am committed to being the best woman of influence I can be as long as I have breath. I love you!

Preface

Let's Take a Journey Together.

Believing that you are a woman of influence, a woman that can change the course of history, for the better, takes a purposeful journey. I am here to invite you on that journey. This devotional will help you understand your influence, remind you whose you are in Christ, and activate you to live within your callings. It will also give you steps to encourage your relationship with the Lord while reminding you of His desire for a close, intimate relationship with you.

As you go on this journey based on God's Word about you, I believe you will see yourself differently, love larger, have new perspectives, and transform those around you.

I want to encourage you to meditate on these devotionals and be patient while your heart is awakened to hearing God's voice over you. You will find that He satisfies your heart, and you satisfy His. When you spend time with the Lord, you will discover He is sweet and kind, and loves us through every step of our journey, the good days and bad days, as we become more and more like His Son Jesus.

I love that you have decided to take this journey with me, and I know when you have completed this devotional, you will feel refreshed by His Word and passionate to know more of Him. He will continue to encourage you in your everyday life. Journal and pray through these words spoken over you, and let your heart be teachable with faith until you realize how chosen you are and that you are here for a very important purpose.

—Katie Walker

How to use this devotional:

This 30-day devotional was created to drive home your value and influence. Start by reading the first five chapters all the way through before beginning the daily devotionals.

Prayer:

May the God of all creation pour out His grace and allow the revelation of who He is to penetrate the depths of your heart as you read. May you be blessed and encouraged to live in the influence and purpose that God has given you. May you be protected from evil, and may you and your family be prosperous in all you put your hands to. You are His darling, and it's time, you know. In Jesus' Name, I pray. Amen.

Introduction

I have learned to enjoy car rides back and forth to drop kids off or run errands because that's where I am able to eliminate all that distracts me, watch the road, and listen. I raise a small army of children from teens to tweens to young school age, so if I happen to be in the car alone, I turn the radio off and talk to God. It seems to be the place that the Lord gets my attention, and I hear His voice very clearly.

Recently, God prompted this question in my spirit, *"Katie, why did Satan give the apple to a woman?"* I was taken aback and responded, "I don't know, Lord." I then waited. I knew that what would be coming next would be a revelation. *"Because Eve was an influencer, Satan knew he could get to anyone through Eve. Women are influencers. You, as a woman, have been given the power to affect others. How are you influencing those around you?"*

Immediately, I started pondering how I had acted that day. Was I kind? Was I uplifting? Was I focused on only myself and my needs? Did I influence those around me for good or bad? Then, a thought passed through my head, quieting all the others, "Wait a minute. Do you really think you have that much power?" That question had a familiar ring to it. It reminded me of how Satan deceived Eve in the garden:

> *"But the serpent said to the woman, "You shall surely not die, For God knows that in the day you eat of it your eyes will be opened, and you will be like God, knowing the difference between good and evil and blessing and calamity." And when the woman saw that the tree was good (suitable, pleasant) for food and that it was delightful to look at, and a tree to be desired in order to make one wise, she took of its fruit and ate; and she gave some also to her husband, and he ate."*
>
> — --GENESIS 3:4-6, AMPC

Notice how the serpent went to Eve, not Adam. She was the first woman and the first influencer. When "...she gave some also to her husband, and he ate it," no questions were mentioned. No disputes ensued like Eve had with the serpent. Adam just ate it because Eve gave it to him. From the very beginning, the power we've been given to influence our world and those around us has always been clear. I think that's why the serpent--Satan--is still very focused in his attacks against women.

Just like Esther, you were made for such a time as this.[1] The power and purpose of your influence have never been more important. The world we are living in is filled with hate, sin, and sadness. We are living in the legacy of those with influence who went before us, and what we do now will shape our present and future generations. God tells us in Psalm 78 that He gave Moses His laws to be passed down from this generation to the next, even to those not born yet. By following His ways, we--as the chosen children of God--will break the bondage of stubborn and rebellious generations.

If we don't recognize and step into the power of influence we have, we will essentially abandon the world to darkness, sin, and the problems this has created. Women are influencers. We can change this world. We need to do so and are called to do so. This world needs you. That's why you are here. We must truly believe the promises of God over our lives, trust Him, and move forward in faith. It's time to discover and embrace all that you are called to be and move in the influence you have so that we can make the world a better place.

May this book encourage you, remind you of whose you are, teach the truth of your identity and purpose, and provide stepping stones upon the Rock to bring wisdom into your everyday life. We believe you will be filled with the overflow and abundant joy that only heaven can bring, and that God will kindle the passionate fire deep inside of you to give you new perspectives on how valuable you are. You are a priceless treasure. Your words matter. You are not alone or forgotten. You are chosen and exist in this world because God said the world needed your influence to continue His purpose for us all: to know Him in all His wonder! Without further ado, Woman of Influence, it's time to discover and embrace the power and purpose of who God has called you to be.

Part 1

It Is Time To Arise

WOMEN ARE INFLUENCERS

*Y*ou have great power and responsibility. Women have a long history of being attacked and oppressed. In both subtle and blatant ways, we've been told what to wear, what to say (if we are allowed to speak at all), what we can do, and where we can go, etc. But here's the thing: control is rooted in fear. We desperately try to control what we are afraid of because then we can direct or suppress its power over us. From what I've studied and seen, it is clear to me that culture has always been afraid of women. Why is that? What could culture possibly have to fear from women?

Let's start by taking a look at some powerful, influential women in history.

CLEOPATRA

As an Egyptian queen and the last Pharaoh of ancient Egypt, she sought to defend Egypt from the growing Roman Empire. She married her brother (yes, true story), who had her exiled. Therefore, she aligned herself with Julius Caesar, who was eventually assassinated. She was restored to her kingdom for a time, but with Ceaser's assassination, Egypt was soon on the verge of a civil war.

So much mystique has been written about her. For example, in *Plutarch's Lives: Life of Mark Antony*, Plutarch wrote: "For (as they say) it was not because her [Cleopatra's] beauty itself was so striking that it stunned the onlooker but the inescapable impression produced by daily contact with her: the attractiveness in the persuasiveness of her talk, and the character that surrounded her conversation was stimulating. It was a pleasure to hear the sound of her voice, and she expertly tuned her tongue like a many stringed instrument to whatever language she chose..."[1] She was the sole reason for an entire civil war in her country. Her image was put on Egyptian coins, yet she committed suicide after she was taken in battle. She affected and directly influenced the course of two kingdoms. She was an influencer.

QUEEN MARY I OF ENGLAND

Queen Mary was the firstborn child of King Henry VIII. She was the first woman to succeed at claiming the throne of England. She spent years fighting for her rights as royalty and is remembered for her restoration of Roman Catholicism. Due to her strict religious beliefs and her persecution of protestants, she gained the name "Bloody Mary," beheaded many, and had over 280 religious dissenters burned at the stake. As a woman, she influenced such support for her beliefs that she mustered an army to fight the reigning king to become the first ruling queen and protected Roman Catholic beliefs. She was an influencer.

MARILYN MONROE

A pop culture icon and a sex symbol in the 1950s, Marilyn became famous for playing the "dumb blonde." Her beauty, success, and fame influenced an entire generation of women, teaching that "playing dumb" is a part of sex appeal. Despite being rumored to be linked with the most influential people of the time, Marilyn died unexpectedly, struggling with reported substance abuse, depression, and anxiety. Today, women still dress like this icon, believing that dressing like a pin-up girl and looking the part will make you the most desired among women. For better or worse, she was an influencer.

ROSA PARKS

An African American civil rights activist, Rosa Parks is famous for her refusal to relinquish her seat on the bus to a white man. Three of the four African Americans asked to move did get up, but Rosa Parks remained. She described her motivation for staying seated in her autobiography, Rosa Parks: My Story. "People always say that I didn't give up my seat because I was tired, but that isn't true. I was not tired physically, or no more tired than I usually was at the end of a working day. I was not old, although some people have an image of me being old then, I was forty-two. No, the only tired I was, was tired of giving in."[2] Her refusal launched one of the most successful mass movements against racial segregation in our history. Her actions have left a lasting legacy for civil rights movements around the world.

She was an influencer.

ESTHER

Queen Esther was commissioned by Mordecai to be coura-geous and go before the king to save the Jews. Mordecai could not influence the king, but Queen Esther could.

> *"For if you keep silent at this time, relief and deliverance shall arise for the Jews from elsewhere, but you and your father's house will perish. And who knows but that you have come to the kingdom for such a time as this and for this very occasion?"*

> — ESTHER 4:14, AMPC

Because Esther laid her life on the line for others, she affected the king and saved the Jewish race. She was an influencer.

DEBORAH

In a time when women had no power or authority to rule, Deborah, under the anointing of God, summoned Barak to gather 10,000 men to go to war against Sisera, the Canaanite general. She believed God, stepped out with her influence, and convinced Barak to fight against the Canaanites who had held them under oppression for twenty years.

> *"And she sent and called Barak son of Abinoam from Kedesh in Naphtali and said to him, Has not the Lord, the God of Israel, commanded [you], Go, gather your men at Mount Tabor, taking 10,000 men from the tribes of Naphtali and Zebulun?"*

> —JUDGES 4:6, AMPC

God went before Barak, and Chapter 5 tells us even the stars in heaven fought the Canaanites, and their bodies washed away in the river. She listened and obeyed God. He used her to influence Barak, and through her, God's people were freed from the evil King Jabin.

She was an influencer.

DELILAH

Delilah is not remembered fondly, but we can see in the Word how her influence changed a giant of a man. The Philistines wanted to overpower Samson. They thought that like the serpent, they would go through the woman. They offered Delilah money, and the rest is history. Day after day, she begged Samson to tell her the secret of his great strength:

> *"And when she pressed him day after day with her words and urged him, he was vexed to death. Then he told her all his mind and said to her, A razor has never come upon my head, for I have been a Nazarite to God from my birth. If I am shaved, then my strength will go from me, and I shall become weak and be like any other man."*

> —JUDGES 16:16-17, AMPC

Delilah used that information against him. She cut his hair then Samson was captured, and his eyes were bored out. His great strength left him. She was an influencer.

WOMEN HAVE DEEPLY INFLUENCED the course of history. These are but a few examples of the powerful influence women possess and how they have affected their families, cultures, and even kingdoms. The enemy is right to be afraid of us. That's why I believe so much effort has been put forth in controlling, directing, and suppressing women. But, we must remember: "For we do not wrestle against flesh and blood, but against principalities, against powers, against rulers of the darkness of this age, against spiritual hosts of wickedness in the heavenly places" (Ephesians 6:12, NKJV).

The enemy has been lying to us from the beginning. He tells us we don't matter and we cannot make a difference, but the early church tells us a different story. During Jesus' time, there was a woman at the well who changed the world.[3] The woman at the well had led a sinful life, but after meeting Jesus, she genuinely repented and converted to the Christian faith. Once she was baptized, she was given the name "Photini," and she turned the place where she lived upside down for Jesus. After she met Christ, she converted her five sisters and two sons, and they all became tireless evangelists for Jesus. At the time, Emperor Nero was brutal with those of the Christian faith, yet Photini persisted in her influence and miracles.[4]

One story of her miracles includes Nero ordering her fingers beaten with rods for over an hour, yet not one finger was broken. He ordered beatings for two more hours, and she walked away without broken bones.[5] She could not be stopped. Her passion to proclaim Christ brought her before kings and nations. It's time to reposition our perspective of women to that of Photini in the early church as portrayed in the book of Acts.

It's time we knew and embraced the power of our influence as well. It is time we stand up in the power and purpose of who we are and walk boldly in who God created us to be. We are influencers. We have been given the power to influence others, and we have been given the choice to determine if that power will be used for good or evil. It's a gift to have this much power, and it's a giant responsibility as each day we decide how we will influence those in our circle.

How will you influence? Will you be courageous like Esther and be open to change if God is asking you to do something that scares you? Will you be bold and confident, always seeking God and answering the call like Deborah? Will you be led by feelings and society's desires like Delilah? Will the power of getting your own way rule the way you influence like it influenced Cleopatra? Will religion determine your choices like it did Queen Mary? Will injustice awaken you to rise up like Rosa Parks? Or will comparing and competing with Hollywood's idea of beauty influence your choices?

Influence was never supposed to be navigated without the Holy Spirit's grace and counsel. Thankfully, we have been given all the help we need.

Choose this day to let God lead you no matter how you feel. Recognize a great gift of power has been given to you. You can make a difference in yourself, your family, friends, community, and even in the course of kingdoms today. Exercise that power with responsibility and excellence.

2

THIS WORLD NEEDS US

It's Time to Care.

*O*ur sinful world is full of hate, depression and suicide, greed and corruption, starvation, oppression, genocides, religious wars, and school shootings.

Pointless and needless destruction is all around us. You hear of it on social media. You see the effects of it and commentary about it on television shows and films. News channels, articles, and videos show us how fallen we are and how much we need Jesus as our Savior.

We need women of influence to step up and be His hands and feet.

The Power of Belonging

Philipa

I'm a screenplay writer, and for one of the projects I completed, I had to dive deep into the character and backstories of Eric Harris and Dylan Klebold, the shooters responsible for the Columbine shooting in Littleton, Colorado, on April 20th, 1999. I found some very startling similarities between them and other mass murderers. One of those similarities was that they all seemed to have experienced significant rejection from women. These mass murderers even cited this rejection as a reason for their hate for the world and the crimes they committed.

I do not believe there could ever be "justification" for these crimes, but I want to again address the influence and power of women. Rejection can influence powerfully. And here's the thing: God does not reject us, nor does he use rejection to influence us. He told the thief on the cross that "today you will be with me in paradise" (Luke 23:34b, NLT). He did not condemn the woman caught in adultery and instead stood against her accusers. He ate with tax collectors and sinners. He was called a "friend of sinners" (Matthew 11:19; Mark 2:17), and He created a massive following that truly changed the world and the course of history.

Do you know how Jesus impacted people so much that He changed the course of nations and the world? He loved people. We are created in the image of God. Therefore, we are world changers, too. We can change the world for the better.

I've personally seen how love and acceptance from women have changed lives. Growing up, there was a boy in my middle school class who, at the time, was kind of scary. He was vulgar, angry, big, and often talked about the weapons he had in his home. Looking back now--after my writing research--I can see how this boy could have turned out, but what actually happened is a very different story.

The next year, a few girls and I decided to be his friends. We created a group and brought him in. He had acceptance and belonging, people that genuinely loved him as a friend and a human being, and he changed. The love and belonging he had gave him security in who he was and purpose in what he was called to do. His fierce personality became protective; he literally fought for us. His intelligence and passion for weapons were steered to a more purposeful degree and job. I truly am so proud and thankful for who he is and to have had such a great friend.

We could have rejected him or even just ignored him, and I don't know what he would have done with his life. I'm thankful we will never know because even when he wasn't that lovable, we loved him. We did what Jesus does for us. I know how powerful and transformative love and acceptance can be. It's part of our power of influence, and it has never been more needed or important.

I'm Sorry Isn't Enough

Katie

Philipa's story gave us a small example of how love and belonging can greatly impact an individual, but we encounter a world that needs this influence every day. How many more news reports of child abuse, innocent killings, or any injustice will we wake up to before we do something?

In 2013, I starred in *8 DAYS*--in a film bringing awareness to child sex trafficking. This was the first time I had been exposed to this horrific crime on a deep level. After much research and many meetings with victims, pimps, and counselors, I was undone. I was emotionally distraught and utterly hopeless in the immensity of this issue, wondering how it could ever be resolved.

The very last scene I filmed in the movie was of Amber (my on-screen daughter played by Nicole Smolen) being brought back to my husband and I, and we see her for the first time since her abduction and abuse. My lines in the script were beautifully written, but all I remember being able to say in the moment was, "I'm so sorry," over and over.

I drove home away from the set and cried most of the way home. I cried every day. I'd replay scenes in my head and find myself in the carpool line picking up my own kids weeping. Something had to be done. "I'm sorry" just wasn't making a difference. I knew I had to do something to help. I began with what was in my hands. The film that we made was a tool right in front of me to use to bring awareness to parents and teens. I could make a difference. And by God's grace, I have.

I've been on a campaign ever since, using the power of influence God has given me to speak to teens, parents, organizations, talk shows, and government officials about this crime. I haven't looked back. Brothels have been shut down. Women have been rescued and freed from sexual abuse and slavery. Women and men have come forward with their own stories of abuse, liberating them from the bondage of years of silence and shame. Men and women have started their own organizations and projects to fight this crime. People have been set free from pornography addiction, which has contributed to the demand and abuse of these victims. The film and issue have garnered national and international attention from talk shows, reviews, and governmental agencies because a small group of committed citizens used their power of influence to help these victims.

All the time and sacrifice away from my family to promote the film and travel to different engagements were fueled by the passionate hope that only God can give. He commissions and equips us to do all that we can to help those in need because He is concerned about the one, the heart that is lost and broken. He goes after the one, and He has given us the power of influence to do the same.

———————

THERE HAS NEVER BEEN a time when women were more needed. What injustices do you see? What tools are in front of you?

God brought the issue of sex trafficking to us repeatedly, and we had no idea what to do about it. However, as we prayed and sought God for answers, He answered each of us very clearly: "This is important to Me. These victims are important. I've given you the tools to do this. Their stories need to be told. If you don't do it, who will?"

Do you not like what you see in the world? Do not ignore or condemn it. You have the power to change it. It's time we are fully awake and aware of His purposes and plans for each of us.

3

YOUR IDENTITY

Do You Know Who You Are?

*G*od has a history of calling up and using the most unlikely of people. Throughout the pages of the Bible, we see that God does not see people the way the world sees us. God calls us by our destiny.

Abram was already an "exalted father," before God changed his name to Abraham and promised him to be the "Father of many nations" (Genesis 17:4-5, NKJV). Despite not having any children at seventy five years of age,[1] God called Abraham by his destiny and was faithful to fulfill the promises He spoke over him through the birth of Isaac.[2]

By worldly standards, Simon/Peter did not appear to be a firm foundation on which to build the church. Simon/Peter was full of fiery passion, but he was also rebuked by Jesus.[3] When Jesus was taken to trial and ordered to be crucified, Peter also denied even knowing Jesus three times before the rooster crowed.[4] Despite this, Jesus called him by his destiny, "Now I say to you that you are Peter (which means 'rock'), and upon this rock I will build my church, and all the powers of hell will not conquer it" (Matthew 16:18, NLT).

The Bible is full of accounts like these—ordinary people called into an extraordinary destiny by a miracle-working Creator God—but I want to focus on Rahab from Jericho for a moment. The Biblical account specifically describes Rahab as a prostitute, which was forbidden in the Law of Moses,[5] and those found guilty of breaking this law could be killed by stoning.[6] However, when Joshua's spies encountered Rahab, she hid them and pronounced her faith in the God of the Israelites:

> *"I know the Lord has given you this land," she told them. "We are all afraid of you. Everyone in the land is living in terror... No wonder our hearts have melted in fear! No one has the courage to fight after hearing such things. For the Lord your God is the supreme God of the heavens above and the earth below."*

> —JOSHUA 2:9, 11, NLT

Rahab proved her faith in Israel's God by lying to the Jericho officials and allowing the Israelite spies to escape. Because of her actions, Rahab and her entire family were spared when the walls of Jericho fell.[7] Even beyond that, Rahab is listed in the genealogy of King David and Jesus,[8] as well as being listed in Hebrews' Great Hall of Faith: "Faith provided a way of escape[9] for Rahab the prostitute, avoiding the destruction of the unbelievers, because she received the Hebrew spies in peace" (Hebrews 11:31, TPT).

James also tells us, "Rahab the prostitute is another example. She was shown to be right with God by her actions when she hid those messengers and sent them safely away by a different road" (James 2:25, NLT).

God knew who Rahab was and the destiny He had for her. She does not have the best name meaning, nor the cleanest past. She was born into the idolatrous Amorite people, but there was a "fierceness" God designed inside of her that caused her to stand up to her idolatrous leaders. It led to the salvation of her family and paved the way for God's people to enter the promised land.[10]

Through action, God showed Rahab that He knew her name, her people, her past and status, but He spoke to her heart, "This is not who you are." And when Rahab yielded and believed in Him, He grafted her into the lineage of Christ.

God knows who you are, and He calls you who you are, no matter how far away you feel from that destiny. God changed and transformed Rahab and countless others. He can change and transform you, too. Despite what the world says about us, God calls us by our true identity. We need to know what that is and who we are.

No matter how we have been hurt, what we have been told, what has happened to us, how we feel, or even how we act, there is a unique and powerful design inside of each of us that is needed in this world. We need to know who we are.

WE ARE CREATED IN THE IMAGE OF GOD

In the beginning of Genesis, God says,

> *"Let Us make man in Our image, according to Our likeness; let them have dominion over the fish of the sea, over the birds of the air, and over the cattle, over all the earth and over every creeping thing that creeps on the earth."*

> — GENESIS 1:26, NKJV

We can never truly know who we are until we know who He is.

God calls Himself, "I AM WHO I AM" (Exodus 3:14), so you can be sure that identity is very important to who He is, and it is crucial for us to know who we are and why we are here. Here are but a few important characteristics of the God in whose image we were created:

GOD IS Truth - Psalm 117:2; Jeremiah 10:10

God is Light - 1 John 1:5

God is Love - 1 John 4:8, 16

God is Infinite - Jeremiah 23:24; Psalm 147:5

God is All-Knowing - 1 John 3:20

God is All-Powerful - Jeremiah 32:17, 27

God is Unequaled - Isaiah 40:13-25

God is Perfect - 1 Kings 8:27; Psalm 139

God is a Most Pure Spirit - John 4:24

God is Unchanging - Numbers 23:19; Malachi 3:6; James 1:17

God is Limitless - 1 Kings 8:27; Jeremiah 23:23-24

God is Eternal - Psalm 90:2; 1 Timothy 1:17

God is Incomprehensible - Romans 11:33; Psalm 145:3

God is the Almighty One - Revelation 1:8; Revelation 4:8

God is Most Wise - Romans 16:27; Jude 1:25

God is Most Holy - Isaiah 6:3; Revelation 4:8

God is Most Free - Psalm 115:3

God is Most Absolute - Isaiah 44:6; Acts 17:24-25

God is Most Loving - 1 John 4:8-10

God is Merciful - Exodus 34:6; Psalm 67:1; James 5:11

God is Long-suffering - Psalm 86:15; 2 Peters 3:15

God Abounds in Goodness - Psalm 31:19; Psalm 52:1; Romans 11:22

God is Forgiving - Daniel 9:9; Ephesians 1:7; Psalm 86:5

God is Just in All His Judgments - Nehemiah 9:32-33; 2 Thessalonians 1:6

God is the Creator - Isaiah 40:12, 22, 26

WE WERE CREATED in His image. Sin has marred us, but it is God's purpose to restore us. You are a co-creator and co-ruler with Christ,[11] made to make the greatest impact on this earth. May God give you eyes to see Him as He is so you can see who you are made to be.

He will be your great defender and the joy in your heart as you learn to embrace more of Him. To learn more about God and the fullness of your identity, read and study the Bible. God promises that He rewards those who seek Him.[12]

WE HAVE BEEN GIVEN POWER & AUTHORITY TO TAKE DOMINION

This is what God commanded us from the very beginning.

> *"Then God blessed them, and God said to them, 'Be fruitful and multiply; fill the earth and subdue it; have dominion over the fish of the*

sea, over the birds of the air, and over every living thing that moves on the earth.'"

— GENESIS 1:28, NKJV

Power and authority are granted. Dominion is taken. Because we have been given power and authority, we must make the choice to take dominion over the changes we want to see in this world. We have been given the green light by God to move and take kingdoms for Him.

"Sonship [and daughtership] is so important that all creation is presently crying out for the manifestation of the mature sons of God."

— ROMANS 8:19, TPT

Our souls cry out to be free from the bondage of corruption, and it is time the children of God take dominion!

WE ARE CREATORS

Knowing that we are created in the image of God[13] and that God spoke and the world was created,[14] I believe that what we believe and speak creates our environments. The book of Proverbs even tells us that: "Death and life are in the power of the tongue" (Proverbs 18:21, NKJV).

I used to skip over that verse, thinking it was a beautiful metaphor or an exaggeration to make a point, but after studying scientific research on spoken words, music, and beliefs, and their effects on water, health, and the human body, I now am absolutely convinced that death and life are literally in the power of the tongue.

Since we were made in God's image, when we speak, we influence and create our environments. That's part of our design.

It's part of who we are. We have been given the power to influence our environments mightily. Jesus said,

> *"For assuredly, I say to you, whoever says to this mountain, 'Be removed and be cast into the sea,' and does not doubt in his heart, but believes that those things he says will be done, he will have whatever he says."*

— Mark 11:23, NKJV

Woman of Influence, what are you believing and speaking? What environment are you creating? You were designed with the power to move mountains. It's time to move them.

WE ARE HIS BRIDE

If God tells us, "Don't be yoked together with unbelievers. For what do righteousness and wickedness have in common? Or what fellowship can light have with darkness?" (2 Corinthians 6:14, NIV), don't you think He would only provide a believing bride for His son? He prepares us and helps us become the bright and shining bride able to be "yoked" to God's perfect Son.

The Bridegroom Jesus loved us so much that He died for us. He was thinking of us the whole time. When Jesus said, "It is finished" on the cross, He used the word *khala* which can mean "completed," "consecrated," or "bride."[15] Jesus finished the work for His bride. You are the bride. He restores, and He finalized it all on the cross.

> *"He who is joined with the Lord is one spirit with Him."*

— 1 Corinthians 6:1, ESV

WE ARE LOVED

Another crucial part of our identity is that we are loved. One of the most pivotal moments in my faith happened when I was sitting in my room watching a YouTube video by Dr. Brian Simmons, the lead translator of The Passion Translation, on his teaching of the Song of Songs.[16] I remember thinking from the deepest part of my heart, "Oh, I wish--I mean I really wish--God felt that way about me. I wish I was the Shulamite woman the King is talking to in the story!"

As I finished saying those words, it's like time stood still for a moment, and the very next words from Dr. Brian were, "and you are the Shulamite. You are the one God deeply desires and delights in. Male and female alike, God is ravished by you!"[17]

I paused the video and cried. I remember saying out loud, "Are you sure? Can I really believe this about myself? It seems too good to be true, and I don't really think my heart can take that kind of rejection. If I believe this, and if this "Shulamite" doesn't represent how You feel about me, I need to know now!" And I cried. I cried because, suddenly, deep in my spirit, something was awakened. This revelation with all its intensity unlocked within the deep places of my heart this truth that was there all along. God was just waiting for me to receive it, and He is waiting for you to receive it, too!

This is part of our identity and who we are.

WE ARE WARRIORS

God is also calling us to be His warriors. Ephesians 6:12 tells us that a spiritual war rages all around us. We will encounter many battles, but God promises to equip and train us.

"Of David. Praise be to the LORD my Rock, who trains my hands for war, my fingers for battle."

— PSALM 144:1, NIV

Hands can be an emblem for relationships or reaching out, and fingers can be a symbol for direction, connection, or giftings. God trains us for a deep, intimate relationship with Him to battle through the darkness in this world. We overcome by His direction, by connecting with Him, and by using the giftings He has graciously given us. Oh, my friend, you are equipped for war.

"Be strong, and let us fight bravely for our people and the cities of our God. The Lord will do what is good in His sight."

— 2 SAMUEL 10:12, NIV

We are called to fight for others, restore hope, and be a conduit for God to use. We must crush the fears we see in others and use what God has given us to carry His glory. Our hearts must cry to wage war against the wickedness and evil we see, partnering with Him to shake nations!

"Now you are ready, bride of the mountains, to come with me as we climb the highest peaks together. Come with me through the archway of trust. We will look down from the crest of the glistening mounts and from the summit of our sublime sanctuary. Together we will wage war in the lion's den and the leopard's lair as they watch nightly for their prey."

— SONG OF SONGS 4:8, TPT

You are a warrior.

WE ARE DAUGHTERS OF THE KING

"The King's daughter is all glorious within..."

— PSALM 45:13A, NASB, 1977

"Now if we are children, then we are heirs - heirs of God and co-heirs with Christ..."

— ROMANS 8:17A, NIV

You have been grafted into the bloodline of Christ. Don't live another day with an orphan mentality. Recite these truths over and over until you cannot help but act like the royalty you are. Being a daughter of the King is not based on you, your actions, or your behavior--it is based on who He is. This gracious King of kings calls you *His,* and you must come to a place in your heart where you call Him *yours.* It is a divine union, not meant to understand, but intended to live within.

"... Fear not ... I have called you by your name; you are Mine."

— ISAIAH 43:1B, AMPC

You are His DNA now, a daughter of the Most High King.

WE ARE NEVER ALONE

The enemy of your heart wants you to believe that you are alone in life. He actively strategizes how he can make you believe this. He constantly reminds you that your circumstances will not change, that you are unworthy, not needed, and have no purpose. God says differently:

"And be sure of this: I am with you always, even to the end of the age."

— MATTHEW 28:20B, NLT

He is with you in this life and with you once you pass on to eternity. He is with you in every trial, struggle, and circumstance that presents itself to you. He reaffirms that you do not need to be afraid.

"When you go out to battle against your enemies and see horses and chariots and people more numerous than you, do not be afraid of them; for the LORD your God, who brought you up from the land of Egypt, is with you."

— DEUTERONOMY 20:1, NASB

PEOPLE CALL us by our mess and remember us that way for years, but God doesn't. People pick out our weaknesses, but God doesn't see them. His love was locked on you before you could even fail. He enjoys you even when you feel like a failure. You are not a problem or a project; you are a partner. He whispers in your ear: you are lovely. He sees the inner beauty inside each of us. He sees us as He has created us to be: made in His image, creators, His bride, beloved, daughters of the king, warriors, and always by His side. This is who we are, how we were designed, and how God sees us.

One of the biggest lies we've been told is that we (as women) do not matter as much, that we are not important. We can be our own worst enemy by agreeing with what Satan says of us. By trusting the Liar and our own feelings of low self-worth, we have ignored and abandoned our identity and who God created us to be. We cannot afford to do that anymore.

I love the words from the movie *Gladiator*, "What we do echoes in eternity."[18] They ring true for us today and always. What we choose to believe and do determines who we become, and, in turn, they affect everything and everyone around us. We must choose to surrender, believe, and move in our identity of who God made us to be.

SURRENDER

"For my thoughts are not your thoughts, neither are your ways my ways," declares the Lord. As the heavens are higher than the earth, so are my ways higher than your ways and my thoughts than your thoughts."

— Isaiah 55:8-9, NIV

You do not have to understand everything. In fact, you cannot understand everything. You must trust and believe in God and His Word. With all my heart, I want to encourage you to say, "Yes." Surrender what you think and how you will look--trust Him, and step out.

Surrendering your opinions to Him will help you see Him in all His faithfulness. The world will fade away, and you will see the power you walk in and how you can influence others with God's grace and favor.

Surrender is about relationship. I know Him, and because I know Him, I can trust Him. To build this relationship, we must spend time with Him, pray, talk, listen, and read His word. We can trust Him because His Word says, "Give God the right to direct your life and as you trust Him along the way you'll find He pulled it off perfectly!" (Psalm 37:5, TPT).

You can trust and surrender to God. The world needs you. You will influence others today, inspiring them to fall in love with Jesus. This love walk has completely changed my world and my thought patterns, transforming my life into a life alive--full of passion and courage. I am a walking transformation because I surrendered.

I have to surrender and choose a lifestyle of surrender daily. So must you make the choice to believe in Him, seek Him, surrendering every desire you have to Him, and then watch the amazing adventure you will have. He says, "For I know the thoughts I think toward you, says the Lord, thoughts of peace and not evil, to give you a future and a hope" (Jeremiah 29:11, NKJV).

BELIEVE

You must believe who He is, what He says, what He thinks, and how He feels. It goes back to what Jesus said,

> *"For assuredly, I say to you, if you have faith as a mustard seed, you will say to this mountain, 'Move from here to there,' and it will move; and nothing will be impossible for you."*
>
> — MATTHEW 17:20, NKJV

Nothing will be impossible for you, but you have to believe it. You have a choice. You can believe in who He is and what He says about you, move in that power, and change this place--or you can reject all of it. God has a purpose and destiny for you. Know who you are, who you truly are. Believe it, and believe in Him. In that, lies your power to do the impossible.

MOVE

The miracle is in the movement.

> *"[Jesus] said to the man, "stretch out your hand." He stretched it out, and his hand was completely restored."*

> — MARK 3:5, NIV

The man with the withered hand had not been physically able to do what God told him to do, yet he began to move and try to hold his hand out. Within the movement, his miracle happened.

That is Jesus. He does the miracle when we move. Do not wait around for your miracle--step out, and trust God to do it as you move. Believe, surrender, and move into your future with great hope. You are a divinely empowered co-creator, an unconditionally loved bride, a conquering warrior, and exquisitely adorned royalty...and you are never alone. You have been given the power and authority to take dominion and change this place. The world needs you. It's in your power to make a difference. It's time to act.

4

YOUR PURPOSE

Why are you here?

J have been asked more times than I can count by many teens, "How do I know God's purpose for me?" It is a question we all need an answer to.

"Where there is no vision, the people perish..."

— PROVERBS 29:18, KJV

People will seek it out by all means: through psychics, fortunes, prophets, prayer, life coaches, and mentors. Do you know why? It is because we have purpose implanted deep within our hearts by the Creator God--ready to be unlocked. He alone does the unlocking and solves the mystery.

God says, "Ask and it will be given to you; seek, and you will find; knock and it will be opened to you" (Matthew 7:7, NKJV). He has the answer. He IS the answer. And, our purpose is to love and minister to Him.

OUR LIFE PURPOSE

He wants to be around you and help you in every single God-given desire of your heart. He desires your attention, responds gently to your broken heart, and fulfills every longing deep inside your heart. You have overcome Him with your adoration. He says to you,

"Turn your eyes from me; I can't take it anymore! I can't resist the passion of these eyes I adore. Overpowered by a glance, My ravished heart undone. Held captive by your love, I am truly overcome!"

— SONG OF SONGS 6:5, TPT

You may think you are not worthy--He doesn't. Even though you have sinned and made mistakes, He still sees you as pure.

"Yes, you are my darling companion. You stand out from all the rest. For though the curse of sin surrounds you, Still you remain as pure as a lily, Even more than all the others."

— SONG OF SONGS 2:2, TPT

He wants your companionship, so lean into Him and rely on Him to correct, empower, bless, and guide you. He says, "I [the Lord] will instruct you and teach you in the way you should go; I will counsel you with my eye upon you" (Psalm 32:8, AMPC).

DECIDE TO SEEK GOD FOR YOURSELF

My seeking-God journey began in 2011 when I decided I wanted to hear from God for myself. I grew up in church and was fed the Word of God all of my life, but I relied on pastors and teachers for this knowledge.

I heard a preacher talking one time about God telling her to tell a woman that she will be pregnant and have a baby a year later. Unknown to the pastor, the woman had struggled to become pregnant for years, and then, exactly as this pastor had spoken to her, it happened--she had a baby.

The pastor shared her story of trusting in His voice and stepping out into obedience. I remember thinking, "I don't really hear God like that. Can I? I'm not a preacher; I'm just a regular woman, but I want to know God more." I wanted to know why I was here; I wanted to know many things.

I still want to know so much more. I am always learning. I decided if I wanted to know this Creator God more, I needed to read the Bible and spend time with the Author. I became persistent in doing that day after day. At first, I did not notice hearing God, or anything really, but I did not stop because I read and believed His promises,

"Draw near to God and He will draw near to you."

—James 4:8, NKJV

He was changing me. When my prayer was, "Lord, see if there is anything inside me that I am hiding from you. Help me let you in, change the evil thoughts in me, and lead me in

your ways," He did. Slowly, the different desires I had started disappearing. He was gentle, washing my heart from the inside out. I didn't know what to pray for, but He knew. I rested and read, and He did the rest. He keeps doing the rest while He refines and encourages me. He fills my anxious heart every single day when I scream out, "I can't hear you!" or "Did I hear you correctly?"

He gave me courage to write this book--a dream I never knew I had because I had been told my entire life by teachers (as well as my own English scores on tests) that I could not write. One of the greatest benefits to seeking God about your purpose is how He can take all those words spoken over you, the judgments from others, and the real cold hard facts from life, and transform it. He shakes His head and says, "That's not what I have ever spoken over you." He is so incredibly faithful. Because of Him, I look at all the impossibilities of my life, then I look to Him with a smile, seeing deep in His heart, and say "I can't wait to see what You are going to do with this!" Give God your limitations and ask Him what He will do with them.

Don't know your purpose? Don't know why you are a certain way, or why something happened to you? Ask God. Seek Him in His word. Pray and listen. He will answer.

YOUR PURPOSE DRIVEN LIFE IS WAITING FOR YOU

Living in your purpose and the power of your influence is abnormal, extraordinary, and exciting. My friend, Vernae, called me as I was driving home from running errands one day. When I answered the phone, there wasn't a "Hello," or "Hey, what's going on!" She presented a very direct question. She said, "What word do you have for me?" Without a hesitation, God's promises started flowing through me so fast I was trying to remember them so I could learn from them.

We laughed, and then she blessed me. She prayed so passionately for me; I was in tears driving home. That is purpose--to be used by God, to be a blessing in someone's life, and to be blessed in return. It's a beautiful life, a purpose-driven life, living with intentionality, living with and hosting the Holy God.

You are powerful, needed, and equipped with all you need to live out your purpose. Begin by studying the Word, praying the Word, and acting on the Word.

STUDY THE WORD

For me, studying the Word began with my commitment to reading the Word. I made the decision to read the Bible every day. I found that when reading, different verses would stand out. So, I would stop and look up different commentaries on those verses or google that subject and listen to a pastor's sermon to find more understanding. The underlying passion to study the Word was to hear God for me. After a while of doing this, I began to know His nature and discern His voice more clearly. This will be a lifelong practice as the Word is alive and constantly maturing me.

> *"Truth's shining light guides me in my choices and decisions; the revelation of your Word makes my pathway clear."*

> — PSALM 119:105, TPT

Through studying the Word, I developed a real and intimate relationship with God and I also learned the power of my influence. To learn about moving in your power, authority, and so much more, seek Him by studying the Word.

PRAYING THE WORD

In my studies, I always wanted to pray in line with God's will. I would stress myself out in prayer with thoughts such as: "Lord, this is what I want to happen; but not my will, Your will." Then, I would fret in my mind about what His will was on a particular subject. I finally realized that I would be in direct alignment with His will if I prayed the Word. So, I began memorizing scripture that stood out to me while I was reading, and I would begin praying that scripture. My faith would build because I knew the scripture was in line with His Word, and therefore what I prayed would happen.

> *"Now this is the confidence that we have in Him, that if we ask anything according to His will, He hears us. And if we know that He hears us, whatever we ask, we know that we have the petitions that we have asked of Him."*

> — 1 John 5:14-15, NKJV

Start today by praying scripture over yourself, your family and friends, and your nation.

ACTING ON THE WORD

The other day, I sat down for an interview for a magazine that covers seven regions of the US, talking about a short film I produced for a local film festival. The interviewer asked me why I had taken another role besides acting. For seven years, he had only seen me on the camera side of films. I shared my story, "I said yes to producing a film because I felt a commission by God to invest my time in the people and story of this project."

I certainly did not feel like I knew what to do or that I had the skill set to do what needed to be done, but I trusted I was hearing God's voice, and I acted accordingly. Being confident to share your story with others is acting on God's Word. He tells us not to be timid. He will do it.

> *"So he said to me, "This is what the LORD says to Zerubbabel: Not by might, nor by power, but by my Spirit, says the Lord of hosts."*

> — Zechariah 4:6, NIV

This is not about your doing. It is about your being. When you focus on being in Him, the doing will happen. You won't be able to not act.

I like to think of it as: what you are filled up with will come out. For my visual learners, imagine you are carrying a full cup of water, and someone comes by, bumps you, and water spills out. If you are full of the Word of God and get bumped, God's Word will spill out. When Christ is within you, you are a mirror image of Christ. Let Him spill out onto others. Study, pray, and act on the Word of God!

Make a daily appointment with God and keep it. You will find your greatest adventure is in His presence. Build your relationship with Him. It is the most crucial decision you will make in this life.

You are an influencer right where you are at this moment. Whether you are a stay at home mom, a professional working eighty hours a week, or anything in between, you have a purpose and a powerful influence. This world needs you, and it is up to you to be intentional and relentless in pursuing your purpose and moving in the power of your God-given influence.

5

LIVING IN YOUR PURPOSE

Influencing the Influencers

*S*tudies have shown it takes at least twenty-one days to create a new habit. It is time for us to create some new ones. It is time to step into who we are called to be and influence the world around us for the better and the glory of God. In this devotional book we have created a month-long study for you. Invest in yourself. Use these devotional days to spend time in the presence of God and allow Him to transform you.

Be intentional. You are worth it. You are needed. Bring your "dance" to life every day. No matter what the day holds, we might have to take steps forward and backward, but we must bring our dance of joy and hope to each situation. The world needs your dance, to influence those around you with God's transforming love. Say, "Yes" to His grace, walk with Him, choose Him daily, and watch and see how He transforms your world! As you read the following devotionals, may you be blessed as you discover with us the power and purpose of the influence God has given you.

We believe with all our hearts that you will experience and understand the deepest love from the Father. We have no authority over what we don't love. This means if you don't know that you are loved, you can't effectively speak life, guidance, wisdom, and instruction into your life or into anyone else's. So, when you want to reach out to the lost, celebrities, or anyone at all, really love them. That is Jesus' heart. No matter what they are doing or have done, love them. Love gives you the authority to speak into their lives and influence them.

Part II
The Daily Devotions

Our prayer as you read this devotional:

Oh Lord, open the eyes of our understanding to grasp the width, depth, height, and breadth of Your love for us. May Your transforming grace and love surround and protect us all the days of our lives. May You rain down Your heavenly treasures upon us. May we seek You and delight in You every day. We believe You will achieve more than our greatest request, and our most unbelievable dream, and exceed our wildest imagination. We believe You will outdo them all for us. May we be the influencers that You have destined for us to be. With You, nothing is impossible. In Jesus' Name, AMEN!

Day 1

You Are God's Favorite

by: Katie Walker

I was my kindergarten teacher's favorite. She asked me to be the leader in class and take the lunchroom spoon to the next class, letting them know it was their time to go to lunch. I remember her always smiling at me. I knew I was her favorite, so I couldn't wait until after class to help her clean the blackboard or wipe off the desks. I anticipated her hugs and the candy jar full of the greatest candy!

No one could do anything to change my mind. If I didn't understand something, she would help me. I was completely secure, gave my best, and was my best. I know I was in kindergarten, but because I knew I was favored, my walk was a little taller, my confidence was a little higher, and my courage was immeasurable.

There is a huge difference in knowing you are forgiven and knowing you are God's favorite. You may immediately think, "I believe I'm forgiven, but there is no way I am His favorite." You could be reliving things you've done in the past, currently feeling as though you don't measure up, or even have thoughts that you believe disqualify you from being "a favorite."

I believe the devil has completely imprisoned most Western Christians today with so much condemnation that it paralyzes us and keeps us from being able to live an extraordinary life, a life of being fully alive. The belief that God disapproves of us so strongly, that there is no way we can be His favorite, keeps us from ever jumping into our destiny. King Jesus has called you His own. You are His bride and princess warrior. Never forget you are His favorite, and there is nothing anyone can do about it, even you! He is God, and He says,

> *"For my thoughts are not your thoughts, Nor are your ways My ways, says the Lord. For as the Heavens are higher than the earth, So are My ways higher than your ways, and my thoughts than your thoughts."*

> — ISAIAH 55:8-9, NKJV

He is the God of all gods, Lord of Lords, Creator of all nations. He speaks, and it is so. He brings kings up and brings them down. He makes a way when there is no way. He carves a path where you only see mountains; He shines a light when all you see around you is darkness. He knows our anxious thoughts, broken hearts, and biggest fears, yet He desires to bring peace, healing, and courage to you. He wants you to walk a little taller, live in confidence, and be brave enough to reach your dreams. He is a tender shepherd who is compassionate in our weakness. He doesn't rebuke us in our busyness or distractions, but He continually calls us His "radiant one."[1]

I heard Dr. Brian Simmons once say, "He knows when we keep Him at arm's length, and He still tells us we are radiant and beautiful to Him." He speaks directly to our rejection and shame. The Son of God looks at you with all your failures, calling you "unrivaled in your beauty."[2]

This is His thought toward you today, right where you are:

> *"But one is my beloved dove-unrivaled in your beauty, without compare, the perfect one, the only one for me. Others see your beauty and sing of your joy. Brides and queens chant your praise: "How blessed is she!""*

> — Song of Songs 6:9, TPT

You are His FAVORITE! Be the woman of influence and warrior bride today who knows she is loved. Walk in that confidence and pour out that same love to others. Remind your children they are God's favorite, tell a friend how valuable they are, and use your words and gifts to bring encouragement to those around you today. When you hear His voice, don't be afraid to step forward. Arise and be brave. When you remember who He is--how He is the God of all nations, how He speaks, and it is so, how He brings kings up and brings them down, how He is the God of angel armies, how He goes before you--you can be BRAVE.

My friends, be courageous. He has a plan for you to achieve infinitely more than your greatest request, your most unbelievable dream, and your wildest imagination. He will outdo them all.

Prayer:

Oh, God of my life, I'm so in need of You to fill me up with Your love. Help me to know I am Your favorite so I can walk taller, live confidently, and have courage to do what I am called to do. I believe Your Word, that You call me Your radiant one. No matter how I feel or what I think, I am beautiful, without comparison. I cannot fail with You. I will walk today in Your love, knowing I am Your favorite! In Jesus' Name, Amen!

Day 2

You Are Powerful
by: Philipa A. Booyens

*A*s I've been meditating on the power of influence that women have, I've been pondering and asking God, "Why have women been so oppressed throughout history?" And God revealed to me clearly that, "control is rooted in fear." He then showed me the image of a collared dog on a leash and said to my spirit, "Why do you put the dog on a leash?" I thought about it and came up with two reasons.

The first is: we do not want the dog to get hurt--we do not want the dog to run away or run into the street and get hit by a car. The second is: we do not want the dog to hurt anyone. Many dogs have attacked people or even other animals. Both of these reasons come down to one thing: fear. We know the dog has the power to hurt itself or others. We do not trust it.

We are afraid for its well-being and the well-being of others; thus, we try to control it with a collar and a leash. I am so glad we are not dogs, and I am so glad God is not a man. Even though we have often proven that, as people, we should not be trusted, God does not collar or cage us. He does not try and control or manipulate us.

Fear is not from God. God is love,[1] and perfect love drives out all fear.[2] However, to our enemy, the devil, fear is one of his most powerful weapons. I want you to truly realize that, "We do not wrestle against flesh and blood, but against principalities, against powers, against the rulers of the darkness of this age, against spiritual hosts of wickedness in the heavenly places" (Ephesians 6:12, NKJV). The master manipulator has been using fear to control and direct culture.

Throughout history, Satan has even used religion and twisted the Word of God to oppress and control various people groups, including women, because he knows our value and how powerful we are. The enemy is afraid of us. He is right to be afraid.

To me, having a history of blatant oppression is proof that we are powerful. There is a reason for our enemy to be afraid of us. So, when you encounter an attack, know who your enemy is. It is not the person or people in front of you but spiritual hosts of wickedness that are deathly afraid of you and the power you possess. USE IT. God designed you to make a difference. You are powerful, and you are here for a reason. Right now. Today. In this moment and season, in this community and country, you are here to influence, to bring your dance, to shine light in the darkness, to heal the brokenhearted, and to set captives free. Move in that, and know that when you do come against opposition, it is simply a confirmation that you are moving in your destiny and calling. Remember, your enemy is a defeated foe.

Read the end of the Bible. God won.

Satan lost.

> *"What then shall we say to these things? If God is for us, who can be against us?"*

— ROMANS 8:31, NKJV

Rise up, and move, Woman of Influence. Light up the darkness and change this place!

Prayer:

Father God, we worship and thank You for Who You are, that Your plans and purposes are perfect, that Your design for me is perfect, and that You are always for us. I thank You for the challenges and victories, and I thank You that nothing can stand against You. Lord, I ask that my spirit come into alignment with Your will and way, and that Your purposes and plans be accomplished completely in me. Lord, I ask for the strength to rise and move boldly and powerfully in all You have called me to do. And, may those around me come to know You, love You, and call You, "Lord." In Jesus' Name, Amen.

Day 3

You Rule Your Feelings
by: Katie Walker

Our entire body reacts based on how we feel. We make decisions all the time based on how we feel. It's a good or bad day based on how we feel. Are you getting the picture? Feelings can absolutely rule our world if we don't keep them in check.

This word has refined me, and I believe it wholeheartedly: "YOU CANNOT LIVE BY YOUR FEELINGS!" Living by your feelings can take you to "crazy town" daily. You must discipline yourself to bypass your feelings and look inside to this question: What am I believing?

Our feelings are based on what we are believing to be true. This is something you must stay aware of and alert to daily. There are days I will wake up feeling down--other times, I'm fine all day then suddenly feel depressed. I can go hours feeling this way; therefore, I negatively influence all those in my circle if I do not catch my negative thoughts. What I mean is, I must stop all that I'm doing and ask myself, "What are you believing that is making you feel this way?"

As Joyce Meyer teaches: "You must think about what you are thinking about!"[1] We must stay on guard.

> *"For the weapons of our warfare are not carnal but mighty in God for pulling down strongholds, casting down arguments and every high thing that exalts itself against the knowledge of God, bringing every thought into captivity to the obedience of Christ."*
>
> — 2 Corinthians 10:4-5, NKJV

The other day, I was really tired. I had many things still left to finish for the day, and I had set aside some time to get it done that evening. The doorbell rang, and a friend dropped by to pick her child up. I could tell something was bothering her, but I dismissed it, knowing I had to finish the other tasks that I had planned.

That's when I heard the sweet voice of the Holy Spirit ask, "Can I interrupt you?" In all honesty, everything I had to do passed before my eyes. I felt so tired. I wanted to scream, "NO!" because I really didn't feel like doing another thing, but I knew I could not let how I felt rule how I acted. I have to trust God and obey.

I looked at my friend, took a deep breath, and asked her what was wrong. This precious friend had so many heavy burdens on her, and she could barely say a word without a flood of tears.

After we studied the Word together and refreshed ourselves on what promises we could hold onto in the Word for her situation, we were both refreshed and full of energy for the rest of the evening. I still smile thinking about how I had so much energy after she left that I could go run a marathon. I finished all I had to do that day with excellence.

Do you see how you must fight your feelings? Had I listened to how I felt, I would have missed out on the blessing from God, and I'm betting I wouldn't have finished my work for the day. The more you study the Word of God and the more the weapons of the Word are inside you, the more you will be able to conquer every feeling.

The Word of God transforms; let Him change you! You don't have to compete for His attention. He loves when you seek Him for wisdom, and He will surprise you with ideas. He will take you on a journey you couldn't dream. Choose Him and His ways today. Say "Yes" to the things you've never believed are even in your skill set, to things friends and family would say, "You can't do," knowing that Jesus can! He makes a way when there is no way. He carves a path when you only see mountains. He shines a light when only darkness surrounds. He is the adventure. What are you waiting for? Dive into the Word. The Word will take you on an adventure of a lifetime.

Prayer:

Jesus, You meet every and all my needs. You direct and teach me like a loving Father. I ask for Your grace to help me always have a heart to be interrupted by You, and to not live and make decisions based on my feelings. Let me not go to the left or the right willingly or unwillingly, but instead, let me be led every step of the way by You. I trust You. I say, "Yes" to You today! Your joy is my strength, and Your Word is a lamp unto my feet. In Jesus' name, I pray. Amen.

Day 4

You Are His Darling
by: Katie Walker

I am so needy. I'll admit I feel like one of the most high-maintenance, emotional humans that exists. It would be unfair to put the pressure on my husband or family to meet the needs I have that would fulfill the desires of my heart (like constant affirmation, attention, or praise). You get the picture. Complete high-maintenance!

Only God can complete us and fill all of our needs. When God does not occupy and reign in our hearts, the world and all its enticements will be a great temptation. However, when I discovered my identity in Christ and began to allow Him to fill these needs, I was overwhelmed by His love, completely captivated by Him. I wasn't seeking my husband to say the "right" words, demanding attention from my family, or trying to compete against other actresses for that "perfect role." I was at peace, full of joy, and adventurously expectant to move into the calling that God had placed on my life.

WHEN I BEGAN to focus my attention on God's Word and seek Him and His Presence every morning, I began to hear things inside my spirit. For example, I woke one morning, and in a soft voice, before even stepping out of bed, I said, "Good morning, Lord!" and instantly I heard in my spirit, "I've been waiting for you to get up, so I could tell you how much I love you."

HONESTLY, I couldn't stop smiling. He does that to you--fills you up with so much joy that you walk around a little taller with the confidence that you are completely loved. God is the transformer. He is the strength, counsel, hope, and everything good on the inside. Are you lacking joy? Do you have peace? Ask Him to show you and tell you how He feels about you, but be ready. It is completely overwhelming, shocking, and all that your heart has ever wanted. It is everything and more that you could ever need. If your heart is broken and you feel it's beyond repair, trust Him to be so delicate with you. He will not leave you. He will not abandon you in your feelings. He will listen, and when you finish talking to Him, wait and listen to Him. He loves us even in all of our mess.

"ALL HAVE SINNED and fall short of the glory of God."

--Romans 3:22, NIV

. . .

TO INFLUENCE WELL, you must know how much you are loved, and you must know this

passionate King that longs for and chases after you. Your limitations do not stop Him. Your shameful ways will not make Him quit pursuing you. You are the most beautiful; you are worth the blood of Jesus, and He cherishes you in His heart.

"LOOK AT YOU, my dearest darling, You are so lovely! You are beauty itself

to me. Your passionate eyes are like loyal, gentle doves."

--Song of Songs 1:15, TPT

CAN we pause right here and let those words wash over us? He is ravished by you-- completely in love--and desires for you to know it! He calls you His friend, lovely one, radiant, and dearest one even before you show signs of being any of these things. He enjoys you and prophesies over who you are becoming. When He looks at you He sees your devotion of love for Him. He sees your life clean and pure, full of grace and balance. He says your words are refreshing and your emotions are in balance. He calls you strong and secure, full of virtue. You are a mighty woman of God, and He wants you to know it.[1]

ASK God to increase your faith. Step out when you don't know where you are going. Keep moving! You must live in the belief that God will carry you. God will give you the creative power to do what He has created you to do. You will be blessed. God will bring greatness in and through you. Be brave and be a blessing today.

Prayer:

Jesus, I draw near to You believing Your Word and believing You love me no matter what I've done in the past or what I will do in the future. My heart leaps with joy as Your words give life to my heart. My soul awakens with delight, knowing You love me unconditionally. May I seek You more and rest in Your peace as I go about my day today. In Jesus' Name, I pray. Amen.

Day 5

You Are a Love Letter

by: Katie Walker

"...Your very lives are a love letter that anyone can read by just looking at you..."

— 2 Corinthians 3:1-3, MSG

I heard a beautiful message from Pastor Dawn Cheré Wilkerson of Vous Church in Miami, FL--she asked, "What does your letter look like?"[1] She taught about the context and content of your life's letter, and I wanted to share a few of the truths that spoke so clearly to me.

As you know, context is very important in understanding letters. What is the setting from which you live? After receiving Christ as Lord, the context of your letter changes. It is no longer shame and destruction. It is now redemption. You are now forgiven of it all, and you are a child of God. God writes a letter in your life, and it begins deep within your heart and spirit. He changes the context of your life from death to life. He rebuilds and rewires what you have torn down, and He restores and heals your story's brokenness. Every circumstance you face has to submit to the context of your life.

Content is also important in a letter. What content is in your letter? What you focus on and what you consume is what you will create in your life. Stop comparing yourself to others, and focus on what God is writing in your life. He writes the miraculous. He reminds you of the hope you have in Him. He showers His great love and mercy on you. Here is a little play on words: be content with your content. Simply be yourself and let His Word transform your own thoughts and heart.

Woman of Influence, you are a precious love letter written by the Spirit, filled with the Spirit, and signed and sealed by the Spirit. When you walk in this knowledge, the world will see the name of the One who has written your letter and that your eyes are open to the destiny that He has planned for you. You are a letter that will change atmospheres, bring hope to your friends, and make a transforming difference in all those with whom you come into contact. May you be a walking advertisement for the name of Jesus today. Your loving Father smiles at the letter He has written over you and cannot wait for all to read.

Do you think the disciples thought that 2,000 years later we would be reading the letters they penned in God's Word? I bet they couldn't even imagine what would become of their heart work. It's time to be overcome with imagining what God will do in and through your life.

> *"He said to them, "Go into all the world and preach the gospel to all creation."*

— Mark 16:15, NIV

Since you are a child of God, called to spread the words of Jesus far and wide, let God write the letter on your heart. Be the "Woman of Influence" you are destined to be, and let your letter go forth into all the circles among which you live. We are desperate in this world to read the letters that God writes upon your heart. Be brave and courageous, my friend.

Prayer:

Oh Lord, You are my beloved, and I am Yours. I believe and receive this truth and revelation that I am Your love letter to the world. You are maturing me on the way to where I am going. Lead, guide, and counsel me, because I trust in You. You are all I could ever want, so draw me closer to You today, and may people see You in the letter that is my life. In Jesus' Name, Amen.

Day 6

You Are an Original
by: Katie Walker

*H*ave you ever met someone that is trying hard to be someone they are not? It's a painful experience. Have you ever tried to be someone you are not? I am willing to bet we have all fallen into this trap. I know I have. I can actually remember quite a few times I've tried to impress people by hiding parts of myself because of insecurities or thinking that they would reject me if I were really myself.

I can remember a time I tried so hard to be so sophisticated, refined, and polished in my early twenties in order to impress people I did not know. I cringe even thinking about it now. I believed I wasn't enough or original enough to be liked or favored. Can you relate?

This is what I would say to my younger self:

"Own who you are. Own every single thing. Own where you are from, what has happened to you, and the choices you have made. You are an original. There is no one like you. Use the past to learn and grow. You can only make a difference being you, not being somebody else. In fact, you only have grace to be you."

In I Samuel 17, a young David speaks to the king with passion and basically says, "Let me fight this Philistine Goliath that defies the armies of the living God. When I kept my father's sheep and a bear or lion came and took a lamb out of the flock I would catch it by the beard, kill and deliver the lamb out of its mouth. The Lord who delivered me then will deliver me now." Then King Saul, not quenching the spirit of this young David, said, "...Go, and the Lord be with you!" (1 Samuel 17:37, AMPC).

Saul had David dressed in a warrior's armor, but when David tried to move, he could not. He wasn't used to them. David took them off, gathered his stones with his pouch and his staff, and took off after Goliath. David, simply being himself with all the grace given to him, killed Goliath and saved the nation of Israel from the Philistines.

David had the grace for victory in his life and actions when he was himself. He put on the armor the King recommended, but he couldn't move. He was able to take the giant down when he was himself.

What armor are you putting on because society says this is the way we fight? What mask are you wearing to fit in with a certain group of people? God has created you to be an original. You have the grace to be the best you. Take on today, knowing you have grace being you and do just that: be you today! The world needs an original.

Prayer:

Oh Lord, thank You for creating me an original. There is no one like me, and You have given me all I need to be me. Help me remember this truth today and help me bring my best self to all those I encounter. You are my helper and counselor--help me and counsel me as I live for You today. In Jesus' Name, Amen.

Day 7

You Are Perfect Because God Made You
by: Philipa A. Booyens

$\mathcal{I}$ started competing in national track and field competitions when I was nine years old. I competed in the multi-events, which meant I had to hurdle, high jump, shot put, run the 200 meter dash, long jump, throw javelin, run 800 meters, and many variations of those events. I was good at it. I soon became a nationally ranked athlete, won national titles, and even set national records for my age group.

But here's the thing--no matter how many titles I won or records I broke, I was never happy or satisfied with myself.

"I could have done better."
"I'm not good at this."
"I only won because no one good tried."

These were words I spoke over myself as a child and teen because somehow I had bought into the lie that good grades, good performances, and good behavior would help me earn a love that could never be earned. God's love--real, perfect love--is a gift that is given freely.

> *"For it was only through this wonderful grace that we believed in him. Nothing we did could ever earn this salvation, for it was the gracious gift from God that brought us to Christ!"*

— EPHESIANS 2:8, TPT

There is nothing you have to do or even can do to earn His love. The "perfection" you may seek, you already have because God is perfect. He does not make a mistake. Everything He does is by design, and you are His masterpiece. Eve (woman) is the crown of all creation, the pinnacle of all that God made, and He said, "It is good."

You are perfection and a woman of influence because your perfect Father God made you, and you need to know it. Spend time with God today. Let Him reveal who He is to you. Allow Him to reveal His glorious perfection and His perfect work, plans, and purposes that include you.

Prayer:

Father God, I thank You for how You love me. There is nothing I have to do or can do to earn Your love. You love me so much. You sent your Son to die for me so that nothing, not even sin or death, would ever separate me from You. Father God, help me to understand how You see me, how much love, detail, and purpose You poured into creating me. Thank You that You don't make mistakes, that I am and always have been made on purpose and for a purpose. Father God, help me to know and understand how perfect You and all Your creation are, including me. In Jesus' Name, I pray. Amen.

Day 8

You Are a Holy Vessel
by: Katie Walker

*I*f you ever want to know what's inside your heart, all you have to do is notice what you are saying.

"...Out of the abundance of the heart the mouth speaks."

— MATTHEW 12:34, NKJV

I'm always on my kids: "What are you watching on tv?" "What are you listening to?" "What are you saying to your friends?" I'm laughing as I type this because I can see the eye roll and the look from them that says, "How many times are you going to ask those questions?" Without missing a beat, I remind them every single day and many times over that the world constantly bombards us with lies. To combat that, we must put the Word of God in us over and over, so that it dwells in us "richly."[1] It is life-giving and fills the longings of our hearts.

We are holy vessels, and we must be very careful and guard everything we ingest through our ears, eyes, and mouth.

> *"Above all else, guard your heart, for everything you do flows from it."*
>
> — PROVERBS 4:23, NIV

The truth is, we will search our entire lives trying to fill the endless crevices of our hearts with all the world has to offer until we turn aside and see what God has been trying to tell our hearts since the day He formed us. We must turn aside like Moses did to see the burning bush. At that time in his life, Moses was shepherding flocks and had probably gone by this area many times. In passing, Moses looked to see that the bush was burning, but it was not consumed. He decided to turn aside to see why it didn't burn up.

Notice this:

> *"When the Lord saw that he turned aside to look, God called out to him from the midst of the bush and said, "Moses, Moses!" and he said, "Here I am!""*
>
> — EXODUS 3:4, NKJV

When you decide to turn aside from the world and all the distractions and call out to God, He will draw near to you! See and embrace how the King of kings views you. May you understand that you overwhelm Him. Understand that He writes a song, and you are the theme of it.

"I am truly His rose, The very theme of His song. I am overshadowed by his love, Growing in the valley."

— SONG OF SONGS 2:1, TPT

You are His lily of the valley. You are made for Him and are the perfect match with the ideal personality. As you draw near to Him, God will take you on a journey with Him. We will learn, and He will hold us up. Get rid of inferiority and insecurity where you watch others advance, and you don't. God told Abraham, "I will bless you," so receive by faith that God will bless you, too. What are you waiting for? Jump in and let the King of Kings take you on an adventure.

Prayer:

Father, we need You. You are our every breath and our every delight. Show us where we let the lies into our lives, and help guide us into Your truth. Don't let us go to the right or left willingly or unwillingly. Tattoo Your Word across our hearts, and help us walk in wisdom. Drown out the negativity, and silence the noise, so we can hear what Your Holy Spirit is saying to us. Search us and know us. See if there is any wickedness in us and lead us to the way everlasting.[2] We choose to walk with You today and every day. In Jesus' Name, Amen.

Day 9

You Can Say, "Yes"
by: Katie Walker

*a*s previously mentioned, the truth is we will search our entire lives trying to fill the endless crevices of our hearts with all the world has to offer until we turn aside and let Him. Let Him fill you. Let Him love you. He is waiting to hear you say, "Yes, I will let You love me and bring me to that place of intimacy with You!" After all, we are held up and together by Him.

> *"His left hand cradles my head while His right hand holds me close. I am at rest in this love."*

> — SONG OF SONGS 2:6, TPT

The left hand usually represents His mysteries (things we don't understand in life), and His right hand usually symbolizes Him catching us. He holds us in all the mysteries we can't understand, and we rest in His love. God lovingly reminds us how well He knows us. In the first four stanzas of Psalm 139, He states He knows who we are, where we are, what we are like, and who He is making us to be. Rest in these promises, and let Him love you!

> *"Lord, you know everything there is to know about me. You've examined my innermost being with your loving gaze. You perceive every movement of my heart and soul, and understand my every thought before it even enters my mind. You are so intimately aware of me, Lord. You read my heart like an open book, and you know all the words I'm about to speak before I even start a sentence! You know every step I will take before my journey even begins! You've gone into my future to prepare the way, and in kindness you follow behind me to spare me from the harm of my past. With your hand of love upon my life, you impart a blessing to me."*

> — Psalm 139:1-5, TPT

Open your heart and let Him draw you to Him. All He is waiting for is for you to say, "YES"--yes to Him, yes to the call on your life, yes to the unknown, and yes to the wait. Before you know it, you'll be on an adventure full of excitement and passion, completely content in who you are. Your future is to display Him wherever you go. Your destiny is to carry the fullness of Christ.

Look at yourself in the mirror after saying yes to Him and say, "I'm becoming an entirely different person!" Christ's life within you is to be given to others, just as Jesus was given to us by the Father. We are to be a blessing to others as He was a blessing to us. We will become a refreshment and joy to the hearts of others. Let Him teach you who He is, what He thinks, and what He feels.

The two things we need most are grace and truth. His presence releases both. Let Him draw you close. We are a nation of people desperate for truth. Let Him tell you everything He loves about you. Rest in Him, and stop striving. He will be everything your heart craves. He will wipe away the fear you don't understand with His love, He will never lead you off the trail of your destiny, and He won't fail you in any season of your life. Let Him be your Helper.

You are called, and you have a great destiny. Dream again, be hopeful, and turn to God. He fills that deepest longing and heals the greatest hurt. Let Him fill you so that you can move with faith today. Believe that the God of Glory will come through you to others. You will be a blessing to your family, friends, church, and community, because the God of Abraham's faith is in you. You are the answer. Go and be a blessing to others.

Prayer:

Oh, Lord, You are the completion in our heart. You are all we need. You plus nothing is the answer. Give us grace today to let You in. Help us be open in every area of our life. Help us look to You in our pain and struggle and just "Let you." Help us say "yes!" In Jesus' Name, Amen!

Day 10

You Can Change Your Perspective
by: Katie Walker

*A*s a kid, I had an overbite, and I'm not exaggerating when I say it was bigger than a beaver. It was pretty cute as a baby, not so cute around age ten and up. Nothing two full years of headgear around the clock and four years of braces couldn't correct! I'll never forget in early middle school; this new cute boy moved to our school. He was tall, dark, and handsome.

Everyone wanted to be his girlfriend. I remember praying and asking God for him to like me. The next day, I smiled at him as big as I could, and he said, "Hey, Bugs!" Confused, I looked at him with a sweet smirk, and he said: "Yeah, you remind me of Bugs Bunny!" I laughed it off and ran to the bathroom and looked at myself in the mirror.

Now, let me stop right here and let you in on a secret blessing. For as long as I can remember, my mother would tell me every day how Jesus loved me, had a plan for me, and made me perfectly and wonderfully. When you hear something enough, you begin to believe it. So, I know the following response was from the precious Lord and my mother's life-giving words.I looked into the mirror knowing and believing what my mom had told me about God, and I smiled as big as I could with all my big teeth and said with a squeal, "That boy gave me a nickname, no one else has one, and Bugs Bunny is my favorite cartoon!" I ran out of the bathroom skipping.

As I look back on this story, I tear up every time, seeing that God taught me at an early age how to shift my mindset. I know the boy was making fun of me; I could have easily taken that as rejection, but I knew my identity. I knew Who made me. I knew God had a plan for me, not based on how I looked, and if I rested in His plan, I could enjoy life. I knew I had (and still have) a purpose, and knowing that kept me from perishing. It is life-and-death knowledge!

Change your perspective. When ugly words come at you, you can stand in the beauty and truth of who you are. The truth is that God sets you up to succeed. He uniquely timed your birth so you could make the greatest impact. You are a child of the King, royalty-- His chosen. He wants us doubly secure in His kindness towards us. He is unfailingly good, unchanging, and constant. It's impossible for Him to see us outside of His goodness and love. No matter what people have said to you or your behavior, your worth does not depend on how well you perform--it depends on Who God is. He puts us into love. He puts us into Jesus, and your identity comes from your union with Him. If Jesus goes by the name "Wonderful", we get to go by the name "Wonderful" (Isaiah 9:6). It's an amazing, breathtaking, and awe-inspiring truth.

God gives us promises we can stand on when we face trials and need to shift our perspective. Whatever you may be facing or going through, ask God to help change your perspective, run with childlike faith toward Him in your need, and know that He responds with His Word--His unchanging, perfect, and life-giving Word. He is with you today and every day, making this promise:

> *"Listen to me, O house of Jacob, and all the remnant of the house of Israel, Who have been upheld by me from birth, who have been carried from the womb; Even to your gray hairs I will carry you! I have made, and I will bear; Even I will carry and deliver you."*
>
> — ISAIAH 46:3-4, NKJV

This is your moment, your new beginning, a fresh start. God changes seasons, and He guides history. Be encouraged--He is all for you! Grab your faith in Him, and take the adventure of your life! It is go time.

Prayer:

King of kings, we are prisoners of hope in Your mighty, life-changing Word. Thank You for Your promises and Your constant, unconditional love. Thank You for the power to shift our perspective. Change us, opening our eyes to see the way You do, about ourselves and others. May we walk out today with a different perspective, a godly perspective, full of joy and peace no matter what, because we fully trust that You will be with us, leading and guiding us. In Jesus' Name, Amen.

Day 11

You Have a Destiny
by: Katie Walker

I had an opportunity to produce a film this past year. I was walking into the meeting, going over in my mind the many reasons why I couldn't say, "Yes" to this project--I have four children, I'm writing a book, and was hosting and managing INsight Scene (a video blog site) at the time, as well as taking acting classes and auditioning. Most importantly, I had never produced a film. I didn't know what to do in order to be a good producer, and did I mention I have four children? I was about to open the door to walk in the meeting, and I was already feeling overwhelmed. In fact, I had already made my mind up to say, "Thanks, but no thanks."

That's when I felt a question bubble up in my heart from the Holy Spirit: "Will you ask Me?" I stopped in my tracks and asked God with a heart poised to hear clearly His direction. In answer, these words burst into my spirit and were all I could hear: "Invest in this person; don't go in there trying to impress them." Immediately, the pressure was off. It wasn't about me. My insecurities of "knowing what to do" left, and I knew the Lord wanted me to be a part of this project.

I boldly walked through the doors, and before he could even speak about the project, I said, "Yes." I laugh thinking how I must have sounded to this up and coming director. I was so full of confidence in God. I blurted out, "God wants to confirm to you that you are doing what He has placed in your heart. You are supposed to write, act, and direct in movies. To prove it, we will go next door and secure the first location."

He looked surprised but started packing his bags to go secure the first location. I sat there wondering what I said and how I could take the words back and run. In my thoughts, I said, "Lord, did you hear what I said? Oh, my goodness, HELP!" I surprised myself, but a crazy peace was all over me.

We walked next door to an amazing building. They closed on Fridays at noon, and it was Friday at 2:30pm. I would not let this deter my faith. I began to say, "Let's look through the window," when the door opened, and the owner was standing there. We explained we were making a film and would like to look at his space. Not only did he let us look, but he also opened his business to us for free for an entire week with filming crews going in and out. I walked to my car that day, praising God for moving and manifesting His favor...and most of all for directing my heart to say "Yes."

Are you willing to say, "Yes," when your thoughts say, "No"? Are you willing to stop and ask for direction and bypass how you feel about it? Are you willing to trust God to teach you along the way? When you decide to jump and say, "Yes" even when your thoughts say, "No," and you choose to trust God--watch what He does. He says,

> *"I will instruct you and teach you in the way you should go; I will counsel you with my loving eye on you."*

> — PSALM 32:8, NIV

Be confident today, knowing His loving eye is upon you. He wants to guide you into all of your greatest dreams. It's your turn to say, "Yes." Be willing to do what you don't think you can do and watch the impossible happen as you let God direct your steps. It might feel uncomfortable, but He knows the future. He knows what projects you need to be involved in. He has a destiny for you.

He will set you up to succeed. You are valuable and needed. Be willing to stop and ask for His direction. Be willing to yield to your own thoughts and rest in His guidance. Your best is yet to come.

As you walk uprightly, the Lord will not withhold one good thing from you. Believe that people will be blessed through your life. You will see things clearly and also see others through the lenses of tenderness and compassion. Rise up, Beloved, and influence those around you to achieve their destiny.

Prayer:

Oh Lord, You are the greatest director we have. You lead, guide, and counsel us. Thank You for the destiny You created for us. Lead us today. Make us successful, open the doors to our dreams, move the mountains, and give us grace to yield to You. May we turn our hearts to You and realize You guide us with Your loving eyes upon us. You don't miss a thing. Help me not to miss Your direction today. In Jesus' Name, Amen.

Day 12

You Fit Into the Right Shoe
by: Philipa A. Booyens

If you grew up in western culture, you are likely familiar with the story of Cinderella, a classic fairy-tale about a beautiful girl that is orphaned and left to the cruelty of her evil stepmother and stepsisters. When the prince throws a ball and invites every woman in the kingdom, Cinderella attends and captures the eye of the Prince before escaping into the night, leaving only a glass slipper behind.

I've always found it odd that this glass slipper is the only identifying characteristic mentioned of the girl the prince wants to marry. Did he not remember what she looked like at all? What's so special about shoe size? Was her foot really THAT small that only she could fit into it?

With this strange identification method, it is no wonder that every maiden in the kingdom jumped at the chance to fit into this glass slipper and thus try to prove she was the girl the prince had fallen in love with and wanted to marry. In the story, many women try to make the shoe fit, and in the Grimm fairytale version, Cinderella's stepsisters even go so far as to cut off their toes and heels to try to fit into this apparently very small shoe.

I'm not sure how many times I've heard or seen this story. We often focus on Cinderella, but God started speaking to me about the stepsisters and all the other women in the kingdom that were trying to fit into Cinderella's shoe.

How often do we also try to fit into a shoe we were never supposed to fit into? Like me, you may have even emotionally or physically hurt yourself in a vain attempt to fit into it.

As I was processing this revelation with God, I felt Him speak to my spirit, "You were never meant to fit into someone else's shoe. I have the perfect shoe for you."

> *"I knew you before I formed you in your mother's womb. Before you were born I set you apart."*
>
> —JEREMIAH 1:5a, NLT

I have always loved fairytales because I think there is something inside of us that connects with these stories. It's how the Author Of All Creation[1] designed us. God knows the desires of your heart; He put them there. His word tells us to, "Take delight in the Lord, and He will give you your heart's desires," (Psalm 37:4, NLT). You are a princess of the King of kings. He calls you, "Royal daughter," (Psalm 45:10-11, NLT), and He has plans and purposes unique to you.[2] This is your life, Princess. Write your fairytale story with Him, and make it epic. You cannot do that if you are trying to fit into someone else's story or vision for your life. Your Heavenly Prince, Jesus, is waiting for you to slip into the shoe He made specifically for you. Allow Him to reveal that "shoe" to you, and step into it.

Prayer:

Awesome, powerful, magnificent, Creator God, thank You for Your perfect plans for me. Thank You that there is a specific plan and purpose for my life, that You have set me apart, and that I am here for a reason and by design. Thank You that I don't have to try and be anything other than who You made me to be. Please forgive me and heal me for the times I've tried to fit into other shoes. Lord, I want to fulfill Your will for my life, no matter what it is. Please reveal to me what my shoe looks like and help me to walk boldly with You in it. In Jesus' Name, Amen.

Day 13

You Are Not Forgotten
by: Katie Walker

*A*fter thirty years of what seemed like a normal happy marriage, my parents divorced. This left scars of heartbreak, anger, pain, and sadness in my life. All that I knew and believed in was simply taken from me. I was already an adult at this time, but it seemed as though everything I knew and trusted was a lie. I was left for a decade believing and doubting in God's ways, His love, and His healing.

I would cry out to God and ask Him to help restore my family, and all I could feel was nothingness and a rage of anger. At the time, I had a new family of my own and decided to focus on that and not deal with these nagging thoughts that God was not answering my prayers the way that I wanted.

The pain I felt was so loud. I couldn't hear anything else in my spirit except this thought: "I will take revenge. I will not let this go for the sake of justice and the protection of my own heart." If I didn't see God's justice, then I would do it myself. For a decade, unfortunately, I wreaked havoc upon family members and my own heart. Every time there was a family get together, I wouldn't go, or I'd show up with a burning rage inside. It hurts even today, remembering the pain. I was so broken. It hurt so badly. For a decade, it never got better, and my heart never healed. The pain was the same--time did not heal all wounds. God had forgotten me, or so I thought.

In 2012, another family event was happening, and the anger and pain was just as fresh as it was in the beginning. I couldn't take feeling this way anymore. It literally took my breath away. So, I sat in my car, and I screamed at God. I said, "Help me! I'll do anything not to feel this way again!" and I cried. I heard nothing, and for two hours I cried and went through all the reasons I was hurting and why I needed to hold on to the anger.

Suddenly, deep in my spirit, I heard, "What if you holding on to this is the reason why I can't move?" In my brokenness, I yelled out, "Take it. I don't want revenge, I trust you. I want to forgive fully, and I want to be released from this bitterness."

It was at that moment something happened. Suddenly, peace and joy rushed in, my heart was restored with a fullness I can't explain, my eyes saw differently, and I loved. I loved so hard the people that had broken my heart. I looked up to thank Him, and I heard these words, "You are not forgotten."

You, my friend, are not forgotten. You are not rejected even if you feel God is not responding the way you think He should. He is walking with you and waiting for you to cry out to Him. In that deep part of your heart, give Him the brokenness and let Him restore you to fullness of joy and hope. God is the The Good Shepherd who never leaves the one behind.

"...for He [God] Himself has said, I will not in any way fail you nor give you up nor leave you without support. [I will] not, [I will} not, [I will] not in any degree leave you helpless nor forsake nor let [you] down (relax My hold on you)! [Assuredly not!]

— HEBREWS 13:5B, AMPC

Whether you feel forgotten or not, He tells us, "...And be sure of this: I am with you always, even to the end of the age" (Matthew 28:20, NLT).

Yield and surrender to His love, and let Him fill you with His fullness. It is life-changing and joy-exploding. His mercy is limitless, His faithfulness is so infinite, and His goodness is unmovable. His judgments are full of wisdom, and His care and kindness leave no one forgotten. He has set you up to succeed! Rewire and renew your thoughts so you can walk out God's great plan for your life. "Woman of Influence," God uniquely timed your birth so that your life would have the greatest impact. You were not created to merely make a dent; you were created to make a difference. Make one today.

Prayer:

Oh, Lord, may we surrender our needs and hurts to You fully and completely. May we accept Your love and grace and walk in forgiveness today. I pray a special anointing of Your healing over our hearts today, so we can walk in the truth that You could never forget us, and You care about every single pain and brokenness we have. Help us, heal us, and hold us today. In Jesus' Name, we pray, Amen.

Day 14

You Are Not Alone
by: Katie Walker

*W*oods surround my home, so when the sun goes down, it is pitch black besides what light the moon offers. We have two dogs that must be walked nightly. On occasion, one or both of my two younger children will walk with me outside. In the really dark patches of the driveway, I will feel little hands searching for me to hold their hand. No one, not even me, likes walking into the shadows or into places where it's difficult to see. We can only imagine what wildlife is creeping or watching, and our history at this home has proven that every once in a while, a snake will show up on our path. The fear of the unknown and our creative imagination can bring paralyzing fear that delays our destiny.

Life is like that, too. I know I would prefer to hold someone's hand and be guided by a strong guardian that knows and sees into the unknown. As children of God, we have been promised that there is a Counselor, Helper, Advocate, Intercessor, Standby, and Strengthener who will never leave us. In fact, He goes before us, behind us, and encircles us.

> *"You've gone into my future to prepare the way, and in kindness you follow behind me to spare me from the harm of my past. With your hand of love upon my life, you impart a Father's blessing to me."*

> — PSALM 139:5, TPT

Not only are we not alone, God imparts a father's blessing. It's too good to understand. It is wonderful and will bring you strength in the unknown, in the dark shadows of life.

My mother was leaving our home the other night, and the moon was full. She stopped walking to praise God for the creative beauty when laying at her feet was a giant copperhead snake. If you don't know anything about this snake, they are poisonous and deadly. They also blend in with our concrete, rock-filled driveway. Had she not stopped because she was led to praise the Lord, I believe she would have easily stepped on this snake that would have swiftly attacked her. Hearing her scream, we quickly went running, and my husband jumped through her car window like Bo and Luke Duke were famously known for doing in the show "Dukes of Hazzard." He flattened the snake doing the Indy 500 around our driveway but not before that snake jumped and tried to attack the wheel of the car.

You see, the Lord knew what was lurking in the darkness. He guided my mom to safety, blessed us all by protecting her, and gave me the best memory and story to retell over and over of how we are a family of snake killers using whatever is in our hands at the moment. Think about it--praise was in my mother's hands, and car keys were in my husband's hands, and I was along for the ride.

Do not place your calling on a shelf and say, "One day," because of fear of the unknown. Jump in the adventure of the unknown with confidence that you have a strong and wise guide. He will never leave you. He is the guide we need.

> *"Seek His will in all you do, and he will show you which path to take."*
>
> — PROVERBS 3:6, NLT

And this:

> *"The steps of the God-pursuing ones follow firmly in the footsteps of the Lord. And God delights in every step they take to follow him. If they stumble badly they will still survive, for the Lord lifts them up with his hands."*
>
> — PSALM 37:23, TPT

Take your steps today boldly and with courage, knowing they are ordered by God. He delights in your move of faith, and He will always be there to lift you up. I speak courage to you, dear friend, to move today into the unknown because you are not alone.

Prayer:

Today, O, Lord, may there be a grace to receive Your great love. I ask for grace to receive this message that we are not alone, and You walk with us encircling and protecting us. We delight knowing that even if we feel alone, we can reject that thought because we are confident You guide us always. We will step today with courage and joy in the unknown, believing You are already there. In Jesus' Name, Amen.

Day 15

You Are Wanted

by: Katie Walker

I was asked by a friend the other day, "Katie, would you rather be wanted or needed?" I responded, "Definitely wanted." My friend was in a job where he was so needed but did not feel wanted. He didn't feel a part of the team, but his talent and skill were needed to continue with the high level of product they were producing. It left him feeling used and rejected.

After hearing this story, my initial response was to march myself into his job and demand they treat him better, remind them who is on their team, and give them a piece of my mind. That is how I felt. However, I've learned that no matter how I feel, I have to take these emotions to God to get clarity and truth before making decisions that could create drama and embarrassing situations at the same time.

Silently, I was asking God how to handle this situation for my friend when the Holy Spirit said, "Tell him that he is wanted. Tell him that he is wanted and needed. Tell him I've created him and given him these skills and talents to make a difference in culture, and no matter how he feels or how others treat him, I want and need him." I reminded my friend of these words and hoped the truth resonated inside his heart.

The truth will set you free, and you must live today knowing you are wanted and needed for this time, this season. How can God reject what He loves? His love for you is so deep and wide that you cannot even fathom or fully understand its depths. We must ask and seek God to reveal this truth to us.

> *"And may you have the power to understand, as all God's people should, how wide, how long, how high, and how deep his love is."*

> — Ephesians 3:18, NLT

At the end of the Song of Songs, the Shulamite bride finally realizes how God sees her, and it completely sets her free from the rejection of others. She is now mature in God's ways and walks in the knowledge that she is wanted and needed by the King of kings. She says,

> *"...This is how He sees me - I am the one who brings Him bliss, Finding favor in His eyes."*

> — Song of Songs 8:8-10, TPT

Oh, my friend, you are the one who brings Him bliss. You are wanted. You are needed. In spite of your weakness and flaws, He calls you beautiful. Know this truth deep in your heart, so you will be able to fight the rejection and lies that come against you in this life. The One who has called you is more powerful than any uncertainty you are facing. God's way is not mere talk--it's an empowered life.

Today, walk in GOD-fidence, knowing He is unchanging! He wants and desires you. It's time to make a difference at your workplace, in your family, and in your community for the better. Volunteer more, take time to listen to others, and remind those around you that they are needed and wanted. Your voice matters, so use it for good in your realm of influence.

Prayer:

Oh, Lord, come away with us today. Reset our negative thoughts with the truth of Your Word. You've given us a handbook of love to maneuver through this life and the lies and rejection that come against us. We believe we are wanted and needed by You. There is nothing this world has for me, but I have all things in You. May we take Your love to the ends of the earth. In Jesus' Name, Amen.

Day 16

You Are Enough
by: Katie Walker

The other morning, I was sitting in front of the mirror applying makeup, and I could see every fine line in my face. Those magnifying mirrors really know how to accentuate everything you don't want to see. I remember lifting my eyebrows up thinking Botox would really help this, not eating sugar would really help these puffy eyes, and maybe a cream would help keep my lipstick from running down all the lip lines.

The thoughts kept progressing so much so that I looked at myself and frowned. I was feeling pretty down about this aging process when my youngest daughter came into the room, walked right up to me smiling, reached out, and squeezed that extra saggy skin on the back of my arm and laughed. Cue the feel-sorry-for-myself music. All I could hear in my mind was, "Your best years are behind you. Just try to enjoy where you are." Well, this thought didn't sit well with me. All these thoughts didn't feel good and started my day off with a mindset focused on myself and all the ways I didn't measure up, and it was only 8 am. Can you relate?

I decided I couldn't live with these thoughts any longer, and I wanted to deal with them once and for all. I spent a long monologue, telling God how I felt that morning and asking to know what He thought. His first response was,

> *"My thoughts are nothing like your thoughts, says the Lord. And my ways are far beyond anything you could imagine."*
>
> — Isaiah 55:8, NLT

I responded, "Then tell me what You think, because I'm really having a hard time with this." I waited to listen to what the Lord would say, and, suddenly, this revelation came pouring in. I think you will be surprised and find freedom for yourself as you hear what the Lord taught me that day.

He spoke to my spirit and said, "The world and its systems have taught you what is beautiful. The world advertises what is appealing to people. You have been conditioned to think once you age, you are no longer as beautiful. But, I created the aging process. It is divine, and I delight and enjoy where you are in each stage of your life. The world will only feed you lies that you no longer are attractive or enough, but when I look upon you, I see where you have been, where you are going, and who you are. I say, beauty is only found deep in your heart's recesses, covered in Christ's blood, and is on display in front of My eyes. I see the beauty in you long before you even show signs of it on earth."

My friend, we are His beloved. We are enough, and He meets us right where we are. You see, I could listen to what the world tells me about aging and what is beautiful, or I can listen to what God says. In Song of Songs, the Shulamite bride talks of her immaturity, and her thoughts are negative, but then she realizes how He sees her as His bride, and she declares this as well,

> *"Now I know that I am filled with my beloved and all His desires are fulfilled in me."*

— Song of Songs 7:10, TPT

We must now be the mature ones in God's ways and proclaim that we are enough right where we are. We must realize that we are beyond beautiful to Him, and it is Him who matters, not the world. We should never fear other people's opinions of what is enough or even our own opinions and thoughts of who we are. He says,

> *"But I will show you whom you should fear: Fear Him who, after your body has been killed, has authority to throw you into hell. Yes, I tell you, fear him."*

— Luke 12:5, NIV

So, the next time I routinely put on my makeup and see the fine lines that have been created by years of life, I will smile and say in my mind that each line in my face is beautiful and that I am enough--as I am and where I am--to finish the destiny that God has before me today. I encourage you to do the same. Fight what the world tells you, combat the thoughts that do not line up with God's Word, and share this truth with someone. Let's free women, including ourselves, from the lies that we believe to be true. You can make a difference right now by challenging the world's view, and reminding yourself and others of the truth.

Remember: your best is yet to come, and you will influence those around you for good.

Prayer:

Oh, precious Savior and best Friend, I thank You that You meet each of us where we are, and You tell us that we are enough. You're the source we lean on, the One we trust, and the Faithful King. You look upon us with Your loving eyes and love everything about us. Help us to have Your thoughts today and to fight the lies of this world with Your truth. In Jesus' Name, Amen.

Day 17

You Are Valuable

by: Katie Walker

*I*magine you are standing in the center aisle of a grand ballroom. There is a royal throne at the end. On it sits the King of kings, and He is watching you. There are amazing, priceless gifts on either side of the aisle. These gifts are all your answered prayers and more than you can imagine, hope, or dream. The King wants to give you each one. You can see these gifts, and they are glorious, but nothing can deter your focus and eyes from the King.

As you walk, you notice your stride is graceful and captivating. The King is enamored by you. He longs with great compassion to give you every gift. Every step you take, the excitement overwhelms Him. In that very moment, you realize you are His most valuable treasure, and you know He would die for you. You long to know what you can do for Him, and without hesitation, He answers your heart's question. He says, "Believe that you are my most valuable possession."

Can you imagine this scene with you on center stage? We need to be reminded of this daily. We are valuable, and we belong to the King of kings. He tenderly cares for you. He loves the grace in your every step as you reach out to Him. You are beautiful and breathtaking to Him. His heart beats for you.

> *"My dearest one, Let me tell you how I see you, You are so thrilling to me. To gaze upon you is like looking at one of Pharaoh's finest horses. A Strong regal steed. Pulling his royal chariot."*
>
> — Song of Songs 1:9, TPT

He sees us as a strong mare harnessed to His heart. He wants to draw you deep into His heart and take you into a new realm. Can you imagine what the King would reveal to you? In His presence, angels bow, demonic princes tremble, our pride melts, and He reveals everything He loves about you.

> *"Look at you my dearest darling, You are so lovely! You are beauty itself to me. Your passionate eyes are like loyal, gentle doves."*
>
> — Song of Songs 1:15, TPT

I always find this so mysterious, because these words are spoken to the immature one. This is how He speaks to us before He has even transformed us with His grace. He says these words when He meets us right where we are, before we even show signs of living for Him or loving Him.

Even in all our sins, He loves us, finds us, draws us, and then offers us real life. His heart burns for His bride. We are valuable, and there is nothing we can do to change His mind. He may not like what we do or how we behave at times, but He loves and leads us out of our own sinful flesh. Remind yourself how very valuable you are to Him, and fight any thoughts that come against that truth.

Your true Hero will come to your rescue. The Lord alone is your Savior. He sings a song over you, and His thoughts of you are so many you can't even count them.

> *"Many, O Lord my God, are Your wonderful works which you have done; And your thoughts toward us cannot be recounted to you in order; If I would declare and speak of them, They are more than can be numbered."*
>
> — PSALM 40:5, NKJV

God concentrates on you. He is for you, doing what you can't do for yourself. You can trust Him.

> *"You've gone into my future to prepare the way, and in kindness you follow behind me sparing me from the harm of my past..."*
>
> — PSALM 139:5A, TPT

You have purpose. You have been called to a purpose, one that only you can do in your area of influence. God has called you and equipped you whether you feel it or not, whether you live in that purpose or are just discovering it. You are needed. With God, impossibility vanishes! Be the breakthrough for someone. Remind your family, friends, and coworkers how valuable they are. You could be the very influencer they need to bring about their own breakthrough. Rise up, and speak out.

Prayer:

O Lord, You are wonderful, and Your love is mysteriously captivating. If I were to search for all eternity long, I would find there is none like You. I am overwhelmed that You call me valuable, and Your heart burns for me. I believe and ask for Your grace to reveal more of this wonderful love to my heart, so I can give to others what You give to me. I believe I am valuable and belong to You, in Jesus' Name, Amen.

Day 18

You Can Move Mountains
By: Philipa A. Booyens

Preschool was out, and my three-year-old desperately wanted to go outside and play. The only problem was that there was a storm outside, and it was supposed to continue lightning, hailing and pouring rain for the next ten days. This was a huge problem for my three-year-old child, but she knew it was not a problem for Jesus. After all, she had been learning about how Jesus calmed the storm.

In Matthew, when the disciples woke Jesus up from sleeping, and they pleaded with Him to save them from drowning, Jesus responded: "'Why are you afraid? You have so little faith!' Then he got up and rebuked the wind and waves, and suddenly there was a great calm" (Matthew 8:26, NLT).

That night, my three-year-old and her big sister spoke to the storm in Jesus' name and told it to be still. When they woke up in the morning, it was. Despite what had been predicted, the storm was still. The sun came out, and we were all able to play outside much to my three-year-old's delight.

Do you believe Jesus and what He says you can do? Jesus said,

> *"I promise you, if you have faith inside of you no bigger than the size of a small mustard seed, you can say to this mountain, 'Move away from here and go over there,' and you will see it move! There is nothing you couldn't do!"*

— MATTHEW 17:20, TPT

My three-year-old took Jesus at His word. She spoke to the storm just like He did, and she saw it calm. You can calm storms, too. You can move mountains because Jesus said we can, and we can trust Him. He made the mountains after all; it is nothing for Him to move them.

Let your faith in who He is grow. Start speaking to mountains, and watch them move.

Prayer:

Jesus, thank You that the heavens and earth obey You. Thank You that You created the earth, and it is nothing for You to move something in it. Thank You that You are faithful and true and that we can believe what You say and trust in You. God forgive me for the times I have not taken You at Your word and trusted in You. Forgive me for my lack of faith in You and who You created me to be. God, I will speak to the mountains and storms in my life and in the lives of those around me. God, I thank You that I will see them calm and move. In Jesus' Name, Amen.

Day 19

You Have What It Takes
By: Katie Walker

I was on a deadline. I couldn't be late, or I'd miss seeing everything: all the smiles, poses, joys, and energy. I had a strong case of FOMO (fear of missing out), and today was no different. The day started early with watching weekend soccer games, driving kids around, meeting everyone's needs, and dropping in at unexpected places.

It was late in the afternoon, and I received a call from my oldest teen who had spent the day with her friends to get ready for a big event at her school. "Mom, we are taking pictures at 5 pm if you want to come." You better believe I did. I couldn't wait to see everyone: the dates, the dresses, and the smiles...but it was 4:45. I had a car full of younger kids. We had been outside all day, and we were across town. I piled everyone in the car, strapped on each of the seat belts and discussed, maybe even threatened, how we had to behave when we arrived.

I heard it all (the complaints and the griping), but I was certain we wouldn't miss it. I was equally certain everything would go as I had imagined in my head. We pulled close to the gate for entry. I realized I didn't have a code to enter, so I stopped just shy of the gate in hopes my frantic calls would be answered or someone would drive by and open the gate. As I waited, the time ticked, the passengers' volume increased, and I still didn't have any answers. I was missing out on the fun and getting angrier at myself. Just then, a car arrived, pulled up to the keypad, and pressed a button. The gate opened.

You see, I stopped just shy of the keypad because I didn't have the code. If I hadn't stopped, I would have seen all I had to do was push the only button on the keypad, and it would have opened with plenty of time for me to enjoy the entire photo-snapping event.

Isn't that just like what we do? We can become so fired up about a project, dream, or event. We work hard all day, all month, or all year, and get weary and stop just before the breakthrough. We just stop. We don't even make the effort to push a little more or grab onto why we began in the first place. We must decide before the weariness sets in to be determined to keep going when we don't have the answer or know what to do next.

> *"And don't allow yourselves to be weary or disheartened in planting good seeds, for the season of reaping and the wonderful harvest you've planted is coming."*
>
> — GALATIANS 6:9, TPT

In Psalm 16, God tells us that His whispers give us wisdom and tell us what to do next: "The way you counsel and correct me makes me praise you more, for your whispers in the night give me wisdom, showing me what to do next" (Psalm 16:7, TPT).

Find your fight in the everyday mundane. Do a little more. Push yourself a few more inches, and favor will chase you down and find you as you rest in God's guidance.

As I smiled, shaking my head, thinking, "Why didn't I drive up to the gate?" I realized I stopped because I used the excuse "I don't know." Don't let this term sit in your mind--it always makes our hearts passive and tempts our will to give up. As favor would have it, the teens showed up late—after me—and I enjoyed snapping every picture, watching every smile, and breathing in the energy of the moment.

You have what it takes to finish well. Remember why you started. You are almost there!

Prayer:

Lord, You are close to me and always available. I praise You and rest confident in You that You will not abandon me. You counsel me and refresh me, helping me to not grow weary in doing well. There is none like You. I could search the world, and I'd find no one who compares with You. Thank You for helping me to continue to move through fear and lean on You with faith. You have given me the best: Your Holy Spirit to lead, guide, and counsel me through it all. I leave my destiny, and it's timing in Your hands. In Jesus' Name, Amen.

Day 20

You Are A Gift
By: Katie Walker

*W*ho doesn't like gifts? There are not many people I know that do not like gifts. In fact, I can not think of one. I was looking at my email the other day and received a film trailer that I had worked on many months ago. I didn't know when it would premier or if it would ever premier.

There are many moving parts to filmmaking, and sometimes the films hit the editing room floor and get buried for years or even a lifetime. To have the opportunity to view the trailer and see the scenes on screen made my heart leap with excitement. It was a surprise gift in my email inbox which I had forgotten about many months ago. I smiled, thinking, "What a gift", and as soon as I thought about it, the Holy Spirit reminded me that "I was a gift." I smiled sheepishly at that thought, almost trying to reject it, when I heard His heart proclaiming louder to my spirit that, "We are all His precious gifts." You are a gift to the King of kings. We were created as a gift and to be a gift to others.

We have a great responsibility once we realize this. A gift is meant to be shared. We have a choice to believe what God says about us or reject it. You are a wonderful gift from God and to God, whether you feel like it or not. God says that we conquer His heart with one glance.

> *"For you reach into my heart. With one flash of your eyes I am undone by your love, my beloved, my equal, my bride. You leave me breathless-- I am overcome by merely a glance from your worshipping eyes, for you have stolen my heart. I am held hostage by your love and by the graces of righteousness shining upon you."*
>
> — Song of Song 4:9, TPT

Live the way you are loved. You are a precious gift to the Lord, and it is time to act that way. You are called, anointed, and commissioned by the King, the One who is overcome by you. You conquer His heart. If you can conquer an unconquerable God, that would make you "more than a conqueror."

> *"Yet even in the midst of all these things, we triumph over them all, for God has made us to be more than conquerors, and his demonstrated love is our glorious victory over everything."*
>
> — Romans 8:37, TPT

Arise and shine, "Radiant One." You are a gift. You are a most blessed gift to the King and to others.

Prayer:

Oh, Lord, may we live the way we are loved. May I walk in my true identity as a gift to You and the ones You love. Thank You for loving me and shining upon me. May my mind agree with Your Word, and may I begin to step into all You have called me to be. You are my greatest love, and I believe there is no one like You. Thank You that I may live in this great confidence that I am a gift to You and others. Help me to live this out today. In Jesus' Name, I pray. Amen.

Day 21

You Are The Theme of God's Song
By: Katie Walker

*I*t was one of those days where I felt sad. Nothing triggered this thought, and nothing was happening in my life in order for me to even rationalize being sad, but there was a longing in my heart. I knew I longed to hear God's voice. My heart craved His encouraging, sweet words. As I walked outside, I began praying and asked Him, "What song would you sing over me right now?" I instantly heard an old Aerosmith song "I Don't Want to Miss a Thing"; I laughed and shyly felt so happy inside thinking God was so sweet to me. That evening, I shared with my Bible study group what happened and asked them all to ask God what song He would sing over them. They responded:

. . .

"Because You Loved Me" by Celine Dion

"What the World Needs Now" by Jackie Deshannon

"That's What Friends Are For" recorded by Dionne Warwick, Stevie Wonder

"Have I Told You Lately That I Love You" by Rod Stewart

"I Get Lost in Your Eyes" by Debbie Gibson

"Wild Horses" by Rolling Stones

"Worth" by Anthony Brown

"You are So Beautiful to Me" by Joe Cocker

"The Last Song, When I Look at You" by Miley Cyrus

We laughed, we cried, and we felt His tender words in the lyrics and titles of songs. He felt so tender and close to each of us. He longed to lavish us with love and make sure we knew we were on His mind. He feels the same way about you. Ask Him what song He sings over you.

The King of kings treasures you. He coined the greatest song of the ages over you. He wrote the Song of Songs from the Word of God divinely with the Holy Spirit through King Solomon, and you are the theme of the song. You are His lily in the valley arising from the wilderness leaning on your beloved. He calls you radiant, lovely, flawless one, and beauty itself. There is nothing you could do to separate you from His great love. The Apostle Paul wrote,

> *"There is no power above us or beneath us—no power that could ever be found in the universe that can distance us from God's passionate love, which is lavished upon us through our Lord Jesus, the Anointed One!"*

— Romans 8:39, TPT

May faith rise up, and the Word wash over you, so you can understand you are His cherished child, daughter, and lover-friend. The lyrics of the Song of Songs will transform your very heart, and Jesus will be revealed as a fiery flame over your heart that makes you reflect His passionate love.

You may think this is too good to be true, but "God is not a man that He should lie" (Numbers 23:19, KJV). He is the greatest lover of your heart. You are the one He loves. He desires to reveal Himself to you. You are the one made just for Him. My beloved friend, when you grab on to this truth of your identity, the eyes of your heart will transform, and you will never look again at any distractions of the world to satisfy you.

Prayer:

Oh, Lord, thank You that You sing a song over us, and we are the very theme of it. Thank You that You call us lovely and whisper loving truths of my identity to us. Help us arise and run away to the higher places with You. You satisfy our heart like no other one could. Help us to walk in Your ways and love You more, in Jesus' Name, Amen.

Day 22

You Are Created to Arise
By: Katie Walker

I had a vision years ago that I've never forgotten. I was standing on a battlefield, and everywhere in the distance were bodies lying strewn across the field. I was standing next to the Lord, looking out and crying for help. He put a flute in my hand and asked me to play music over them. As the sweet melody of the sound began to play, the dead bodies began to wake up. I was so excited that I began jumping and running and playing the melody over as many as I could.

The Holy Spirit began explaining that the dead were my brothers and sisters who have grown weary in the battle. Many had grown tired and delay brought discouragement. The enemy had ravaged the church destroying many in the fight. Most all had given up because of the wounds inflicted upon them. He explained that as we display our love for Jesus (representing playing the music), it would awaken and refresh the soldiers in the battle. I knew then He wanted us to arise, and a revival of love for the King within our heart was the answer. Song of Songs tells us,

"For your kisses of love are exhilarating, more than any delight I've known before. Your kisses of love awaken even the lips of sleeping ones."

— SONG OF SONGS 7:9, TPT

As we display our love of Jesus, we will awaken even the lips of the sleeping ones.

As you fall in love with Jesus, God will conquer all the plans coming against you. You must lean into Him, and He will take your hand as you take steps into all the plans He has for you. This will be an epic dance with the King, where He will establish you. His love will overshadow you, and He will lead, guide, and counsel you.

You must take heart. The enemy looks big, but God is bigger. The enemy looks powerful, but God is more powerful. The "Great I Am" will take you further than you ever imagined. He will show you in the night, the strategic plans to follow. He will reveal hidden mysteries for you to release. He will be your mouthpiece and power. Just say, "Yes." Say, "Yes," and you will dance. What a show! What a marvelous show of love that will be displayed.

"So now wrap your heart tightly around the hope that lives within us, knowing that God always keeps his promises!"

— HEBREWS 10:23, TPT

Prayer:

Oh, Lord, You are our great love. We are lovesick for You in this weary wilderness. We thirst with deepest longings to love You more. Your tender mercies are new each day, and we passionately love You with all our hearts. Blow on us until we are fully Yours. May we walk with You as Adam did in the paradise garden, in Jesus' Name. Amen.

Day 23

You Can Repent
By: Philipa A. Booyens

*T*here is not one among us who is without sin. There is not one among us who could cast the first stone. We have all fallen short of the glory of God and need grace. We need a savior, and no matter how far we have fallen or how much we have done, we can always repent. He promises to forgive us, and "God is not a man that he should lie" (Numbers 23:19, KJV).

For over a year now II Chronicles 7:14 has been burning in my heart:

> *"If My people who are called by My name will humble themselves, and pray and seek My face, and turn from their wicked ways, then I will hear from heaven, and will forgive their sin and heal their land."*

— II Chronicles 7:14, NKJV

I saw a vision last year that bothered me greatly, but I believe it is relevant for us in this time. In January of 2019, New York passed The Reproductive Health Act, expanding abortion rights and eliminating several restrictions within the state. It received national attention, and in honor of the bill's passing, the One World Trade Center was lit pink.

Numerous political and pastoral opponents to the bill cried out, "Blood is on their hands," and as I read their laments, I was immediately impressed with the words, "If blood is on their hands, then it is on ours as well."

Then, I was taken into a vision. I saw myself kneeling in a flood of blood. It stretched out as far as I could see, about a foot deep, covering the ground. I was kneeling in this blood, covered in it from head to toe. It was dripping from my hair to the ground, and as I held out my blood-covered hands and stared at them in despair and horror, I thought, "What have I done?"

This has bothered me a lot. I love Jesus. I always try to follow Him and do the right thing, but I saw and felt my guilt so clearly in that moment. I knew we all carried the same guilt because these are the leaders we have elected. They represent us. We have allowed abortion laws and procedures by not speaking up, not helping out, and not praying fervently.

Convicted by what I saw, I started praying, researching, and seeking counsel. The Bible tells us that spilled blood cries out, and God hears it. We see this clearly in Genesis 4 when Cain murdered his brother Abel:

"And He [God] said, "What have you done? The voice of your brother's blood cries out to Me from the ground."

— GENESIS 4:10, NKJV

In response to the vision, Ezekiel 33 was given to me by a mentor, and its warning has haunted me ever since:

> *"The word of the Lord came to me: "Son of man, speak to your people and say to them: 'When I bring the sword against a land, and the people of the land choose one of their men and make him their watchman, and he sees the sword coming against the land and blows the trumpet to warn the people, then if anyone hears the trumpet but does not heed the warning and the sword comes and takes their life, their blood will be on their own head. Since they heard the sound of the trumpet but did not heed the warning, their blood will be on their own head. If they had heeded the warning, they would have saved themselves. But if the watchman sees the sword coming and does not blow the trumpet to warn the people and the sword comes and takes someone's life, that person's life will be taken because of their sin, but I will hold the watchman accountable for their blood.'"*

> — EZEKIEL 33:1-6, NIV

I've seen and heard the blood on my hands, so I have repented, and, now, I must warn you. God heard the blood crying from the ground after just one murder. How much more so the blood from over 60 million babies since Roe v. Wade was passed? That much blood would cover the ground like a flood.

This is just one issue. It is time to humble ourselves and turn from our wicked ways. It is time to repent so that God may hear from Heaven and heal our land.[1] The blood is crying out. The blood is on our hands. We must do something. We must be the ones to fight for God's ways and for God's Kingdom to reign on this earth. You were made for this moment to be the one who stands in the gap and changes the very trajectory for the generations behind us.

God has given us authority, and it's time to take dominion. We must search our hearts, repent, and ask God's forgiveness, and then move like the women of influence God called us to be. We need to take His glory to the nations so His ways will be known throughout the earth. Let's change this world by humbling our hearts in repentance, praying fervently, and helping people in need. The time is now, and it is up to us!

Prayer:

Jesus, I repent for all the times and all the things I have not paid attention to or spoken up about. Lord, I repent for walking by my neighbors and not helping. Lord, I repent for our leaders that have allowed the spilling of blood. Oh, Father God, I repent. Have mercy on us. Thank You for Your forgiveness. Thank You for loving us so much that You died for all of us, once and for all. Thank You that nothing we have done, or ever will do, is too much for Your blood to cover. Lord, I bless Your name, the name above all names, and I thank You. In Jesus' Name, I pray. Amen.

Day 24

You Have A Merciful Father God
By: Philipa A. Booyens

My little brother got away with nearly everything. He's always been adventurous and fun, but I remember my grandmother telling him, "Those hands are going to get you in trouble," and they often did. Like many children, my little brother got into a lot of trouble, but he quickly learned how to admit his guilt (what he did wrong), say sorry (repent), and appeal for mercy from our parents, and he almost always got it.

Growing up as a rule-following, firstborn child seeing this play out, I must've said something to the effect of "that's not fair" quite often because I distinctly remember my mother reinforcing: "Life isn't fair, and you don't want it to be." As my mother, she likely recognized and wanted me to realize that no matter how many rules I followed or how well I performed, I still needed mercy, too.

We need to recognize and be thankful for this mercy which comes from our Father God's great love for us. The book of Jonah illustrates this so well for us. Scripture tells us that the city of Nineveh was so wicked that God told the prophet Jonah to go warn them that their city would be overthrown in forty days. When Jonah ran away from what God called him to do, God went so far as to send a great wind on the sea and prepared a great fish swallow Jonah up in order to get him back to Nineveh. God showed great mercy to Jonah in saving him from the storm and spitting him out of the great fish, but He also showed great mercy to the people of Nineveh to go to such lengths to warn them. In their wickedness, they deserved to be overthrown and destroyed. Jonah definitely thought so. However, when the people of Nineveh repented, God spared all of them.

> *"When God saw what they did and how they turned from their evil ways, he relented and did not bring on them the destruction he had threatened."*

> —JONAH 3:10, NIV

Life isn't fair. Thank God for it. We must be thankful we don't get what we deserve, because we do have a merciful, loving Father God that consistently goes out of His way and wants us to appeal for mercy from Him because He loves us.

Today, allow God to reveal Himself as the merciful Father. Allow Him to show you where He has been merciful to you, and thank Him.

Prayer:

Father God, thank You, thank You, thank You for how You have loved me and given me mercy even if, and especially when, I didn't deserve it. Thank You that You are a merciful Father Who loves His children. Lord, help me to forgive and not hold onto any anger when You are merciful to others even when they do not deserve it. Lord, help me to see any way I have been disobedient to You. I don't want to walk in any way that hurts Your heart. Lord, for these things I repent and ask for mercy. Thank You for Your forgiveness. You are so, so good, and I am so in love with You. In Jesus' Name, I pray. Amen.

Day 25

You Have A Restorer
By: Katie Walker

*T*his is a new day and new beginning, and it is time for restoration and awakening. Let the Word of God get deep inside your heart so that when trials and temptations come your way, you will be a walking pillar of strength, making good decisions full of wisdom. There is rich revelation in the Word of God beneath the surface. God says He "will extend His hand to restore."

> *"On that day, the Lord will extend his hand a second time to restore the remnant of his people from Assyria, Egypt, Pathros, Ethiopia, Iran, Iraq, Syria, and the coastlands of the sea."*

— Isaiah 11:11, TPT

He is the God of restoration. He will restore those that have failed Him miserably. That is all of us! We don't have to strive or work for the restoration. We only have to believe and obey His word. He is extending His hand to you today. We just get to take His hand and let Him restore us.

Let's unpack the gold in these verses today. There are eight different regions in this verse. These are eight regions in our heart that Christ wants to restore in us. The number eight always stands for "new beginnings," so there are eight new beginnings God wants to restore within your heart. Let's look at a few of the regions.

Pathros is a region in upper Egypt that means "desert dryness."[1] God wants to extend His hand and restore the dryness in your life. You must determine in your heart that God wants to restore those areas, so self-pity cannot babysit you anymore. It's time to get up, knowing you can grab Him by the hand and let Him water you in His Word.

Ethiopia or Cush means "scorched or blackened."[2] God will restore the blackened parts of your heart. He will "... give them a beautiful bouquet in the place of ashes, the oil of bliss instead of tears, and the mantle of joyous praise instead of the spirit of heaviness" (Isaiah 61:3, TPT).

Iran means "the hidden or concealed places of your heart."[3] We have so many areas that we hide from others because of shame, but God wants to restore those places you don't like. He loves you and wants to meet you where you are and restore every hidden place to make them new.

Iraq means "divided land or divided stream."[4] How many times is our heart divided, where we are standing with one foot in the world and one foot in the Word of God? This shouldn't be so, and He says He will extend His hand to you and pull you into a new place of pure, undiluted devotion to Him and Him alone.

Syria means "walled up fortress."[5] There are many hurts and rejections that happen in life that cause us to build walls around our heart for protection. God will melt your walls and restore that part of your heart so that you can know true love.

Remind yourself that God says He will restore those regions in your heart where you are struggling. All you have to do is take His hand and lean entirely on Him and His faithfulness. This is a new day and a new beginning. Let the King of all, who is faithful and true, joyfully teach you and be your Restorer.

Prayer:

Oh, Lord, You are our Way-maker, Miracle Worker, and Hero Defender. Thank You for moving the mountains in our life for us. Thank You for making a way where there is no way. Thank You for restoring us over and over again. Thank You that we can walk strong and victorious and full of wisdom because You are our Strength and Restorer. Thank You that You pour out a father's blessing upon us. As we dive into the Word and become a follower of Christ, You speak tenderly to us, restoring the regions in our heart to a brand new beginning. Thank You! May we give all of our burden to You and know that You are True and Faithful. In Jesus' Name, we pray. Amen.

Day 26

You Are Free
by: Katie Walker

I'll never forget in early childhood, I came home from school one time with minus points on my paper because I had drawn animals and the world we live in using colors that were not real-life. I had colored a giraffe purple, the dirt blue, and everything else you can think of--as unrealistic as possible. I was devastated by this grade. I am a people pleaser by nature, and minus points just about ruined my life at the time. Not to mention, that one act instilled limits on my creativity. From then on, every picture or story I would write was real-life or what I knew to be real-life. Writing was a struggle, and drawing pictures ceased. I was uninterested in creating in school, and so my playground became imaginary worlds, and I would pretend for hours in my backyard.

In hindsight, this one act was a blessing in disguise, because the world of the imaginary must be cultivated to do what I do now. However, I want to point out that we do need the freedom to create. Even though I stopped creating on paper, I still created in my mind. In my mind, I could be free! You will never be free until you understand and believe that you are free. God tells us we are free. What does that actually mean?

> *"For the law of the Spirit of life in Christ Jesus has made me free from the law of sin and death."*

— ROMANS 8:2, NKJV

Believing in Jesus Christ, declaring Him to be your Lord, and inviting Him in your life is freedom. It is a belonging (apart from this world), a security of eternal truth, and an ever-present friend at all times. At that moment, you become alive. A new breath, fresh heart, and new life is your future.

The bondage of the world's rules no longer applies to you. Depression, shame, regret, and illness are just a few things that must go. He gives you the power to overcome obstacles and bad behaviors of the past. God allows you, without hindrance, to grab hold of a brand-new life in Him. You become holy and desire to catch all the foxes that try to destroy the relationship between you and God.

> *"You must catch the troubling foxes, those sly little foxes that hinder our relationship. For they raid our budding vineyard of love to ruin what I've planted within you. Will you catch them and remove them for me? We will do it together."*

— SONG OF SONGS 2:15, TPT

We all have different compromises in our lives where we
haven't allowed God to enter and change us. These "foxes"
keep the fruit of the Spirit from growing in us and keep us
from experiencing freedom in our lives. Once we are His, He
frees us completely from our sin and everything that entangles
us. He gives us life with His mercy and grace ushering us into
true freedom and the destiny He has planned for us. This
means your best is yet to come. You are not enslaved to
anything or anyone. You are a courageous champion jumping
into the calling He has on your life without fear. You may feel
fear, but you must rely on His heart and not what you feel.
You have a new relationship now, and you must understand,

*"I know my lover is mine, and I have everything in you, for we delight
ourselves in each other."*

— SONG OF SONGS 2:16, TPT

The One Who delights in you wants you to live without
hindrance or restraint. You are free to create your destiny. You
may think you are unable to go for your dream, but, my
friend, we were all unable. God will raise you up with His
mighty strength and power, and you will be the "Woman of
Influence" you were created to be to awaken those around
you. Your past doesn't matter. It ended with three nails. You
only have a destiny--walk in it today. Take those around you
by the hand and escort them into their destiny as well. You
have the power. Go and be.

Prayer:

*Oh, Lord, may we know within our deepest heart how we are free, how
You've conquered sin and death for us by the blood of Jesus, and how You
desire us to live life differently in this world. We are to live free from all*

that holds us captive and steals our joy. Help us to see and also create heaven on earth releasing Your glory. May we shine like You and live in the freedom to which You have called us. In Jesus' Name, we pray. Amen.

Day 27

You Are A Message
by: Katie Walker

hen my family vacations, we love to search for sand crabs as the sun goes down on the beach. We always carry flashlights, nets, and buckets and have fun competitions on who can catch the biggest crab. On one particular vacation, my youngest child (who is highly competitive) took off running across the beach, leaving me trailing along from behind. I saw her searching for a while with no luck and then a moment later chasing a crab. She turned around with a huge smile and yelled, "Mom, I prayed and asked God to help me find a big crab and look!" There in her bucket was the largest sand crab I've ever seen. Our excitement drew some other beachgoers and small children. A younger little boy came running to see the crab. His eyes were as big as saucers and he asked how we found this crab. We were able to share that my daughter had prayed and God gave her this crab. We asked him if he wanted this big crab because we knew that this little boy would also testify that God found this crab for him.

Your story needs to be told.

There is a similar story in the Bible of a demon-filled man getting set free. God not only set this man free because He loves him, but He knew that his story would set others free as well. This demon-filled man had many demons inside of him, and he was forced to live outside the city in the graveyard because he was insane. Jesus arrived on the scene and delivered him from the mob of demons. The delivered man wanted to leave the city and follow Jesus, but Jesus wanted him to go tell his story.

> *"But the man who had been set free begged Jesus over and over not to leave, saying, "Let me be with you!" Jesus sent him away with these instructions: "Return to your home and your family, and tell them all the wonderful things God has done for you." So the man went away and preached to everyone who would listen about the amazing miracle Jesus had worked in his life.*
>
> — Luke 8:38-39, TPT

This man's voice mattered. This man would carry a message of miracles to others. If you have asked Jesus in your heart to be your Savior, you have experienced a miracle. He is a transforming Glory that moves through you to the world around you.

Are you telling others about the miracles that God has done for you? Has God freed you in certain areas? Do you need freeing in other areas? Is there something in your life that is stopping the flow of God in your life?

You are an image-bearer and a co-creator with Christ, and you are made for this very moment to make the greatest impact on this earth. We walk with Christ so we can co-create with Him. When you begin to testify about your miracles and what God has done for you, you free others by building their faith to believe that God will do it for them as well. He wants to free your voice. He wants you to go! He is with you, walking with you, and it is time to take authority with your story that God has given you. As you step out in faith, the miracles begin.

They don't begin as you wait, but when you move. Create the atmosphere of Christ right where you are and bring Heaven's Kingdom to earth.

Prayer:

Lord, we love You and thank You that we are co-creators with You. Thank You that You call us image-bearers and that You walk with us through every storm. Thank You that You are covering us as we move into the unknown with You. Thank You for giving us the courage to speak and testify of Your goodness and miracles. Give us opportunities today to see who we can share our testimony of You with, and touch our words that they bring encouragement, displaying who You are. May we be overwhelmed by Your love today so that we can overwhelm others with Your love, bringing Your glory to those in our path. Create within us in Jesus' Name. Amen.

Day 28

You Are An Ambassador
by: Katie Walker

I, along with my team at After Eden Pictures, had the greatest opportunity to visit the United States Embassy in the Dominican Republic while traveling and promoting the 8 DAYS film. The US Government partnered together with the Dominican Republic to bring awareness to the crime of sex trafficking by having us tour and speak throughout the country on this uncomfortable topic.

After experiencing this visit with the Ambassador at the Embassy, I couldn't help but compare their life with the life we have as Christ's ambassadors.

"So we are Christ's ambassadors, God making His appeal as it were through us. We [as Christ's personal representatives] beg you for His

sake to lay hold of the divine favor [now offered you] and be reconciled to God."

— 2 CORINTHIANS 5:20, AMPC

These are a few of the similarities we are blessed to have in your position as an Ambassador of Christ:

- The US ambassador had a direct line of contact with the President of the United States, and we have direct contact through our Savior, Jesus Christ, with God Almighty.

  "For through Him we both have access by one Spirit to the Father."

  — EPHESIANS 2:18, NKJV

- The ambassador had secret service protection everywhere they traveled and stayed while living in the foreign land. Likewise, we can always come to the mercy seat of Christ and rest without fear, for He will hide, protect, and be our refuge in this world.

  "His massive arms are wrapped around you, protecting you. You can run under his covering of majesty and hide. His arms of faithfulness are a shield keeping you from harm. You will never worry about an attack of demonic forces at night nor have to fear a spirit of darkness coming against you."

  — PSALM 91:4-5, TPT

- The Ambassador of the United States helped aid Americans living and traveling outside the United States. We, as Ambassadors of Christ, have the perfect message with the perfect Messiah to help aid and bring hope to the broken and backsliding.

"For by grace you have been saved through faith, and not of yourselves; It is the gift of God, not of works, lest anyone should boast. For we are His workmanship, created in Christ Jesus for good works, which God prepared beforehand that we should walk in them."

— EPHESIANS 2:8-10, NKJV

- Lastly, while living in a foreign country, the United States Ambassadors are given a beautiful home and an interpreter in order to maneuver easily in the foreign country. Similarly, we have been given the beautiful Holy Spirit to indwell us and interpret all of our needs.

"But the Helper, the Holy Spirit, whom the Father will send in My name, He will teach you all things, and bring to your remembrance all things that I said to you."

—JOHN 14:26, NKJV

BE bold today in the way you walk, talk, and conduct yourself, reminding yourself you are an ambassador of the One Who provides for us. God plus nothing equals all we need. He is our Counselor in good and bad situations; our Helper for all things; our Advocate, always having our back; our Intercessor, praying on our behalf; our Strengthener, building muscles to finish this race well; and our Constant Companion, never leaving our side.

Be courageous today!

Prayer:

Precious Holy Spirit, You are more wonderful than we can imagine. You direct us to Christ and pour truth into our hearts. Help us be the mirror image of Christ, that when people look to us today, we could radiate the glory of the risen Savior. Thank You for all of the privileges and blessings of being an Ambassador of Christ. Help us to recognize this favor, walk in it daily, and represent You by Your grace. In Jesus' Name, we pray. Amen.

Day 29

You Can Write Your Own Story
by: Philipa A. Booyens

*O*ur words are powerful things. The Word of God tells us that,

"Your words are so powerful that they will kill or give life, and the talkative person will reap the consequences."

— PROVERBS 18:21, TPT

God spoke, and the world was created. We are created in His likeness and image, which means our words create, too.

Writers know the power of their words and can create powerful stories that move us and change the way we view the world and interact with the people in it. As a writer, I believe this is one of the most powerful things our words can do. We can create stories and build worlds out of nothing. Have you ever stared at a blank sheet of paper or a blank word document or note? It's open. It's blank and full of possibilities, and when we string ordinary letters and words together, we can create anything.

I want you to start to see your life as a great epic story. I want you to see every new day as a blank page. Nothing has been written on it yet, and no matter what has happened before, today is blank. You get to write on it with every decision you make.

> *"Today I have given you the choice between life and death, between blessings and curses. Now I call on heaven and earth to witness the choice you make. Oh, that you would choose life, so that you and your descendants might live!"*
>
> — DEUTERONOMY 30:19, NLT

With every decision you make, you choose who you become and where you will go. Choose life. Write your story with God. It's going to be epic.

Prayer:

Lord God, thank You that You are the Living Word made flesh. Thank You for creating us, our world, and everything in it out of nothing. Thank You that it brought You great joy and that it is good. We worship You and praise You and thank You for that. Lord God, thank You for creating us in Your image. Thank You for giving us power to create with our words and to write our stories with our choices. Help me to realize how powerful that is. Lord, I want to write my story with You today and every day forward.

Thank You for having plans and purposes for me that give me a hope and a future. Thank You for my life. Let's write an epic story together. In Jesus' Name, I pray. Amen.

Day 30

You Are Royalty
by: Katie Walker

I can remember as a child playing pretend constantly. We lived in a two-story home, and I would pretend to be the queen of a great nation that was attacked by an evil king. I would be held as a prisoner until the handsome prince would come and save me. I'm sure I stole most of my stories from Disney somewhere between Rapunzel and Cinderella, but there was a constant theme. I was always a princess, and I was always royalty.

Little did I know as a child that this is our true calling and rightful inheritance. It is who we are. It is what God calls us. He places a crown on our head and watches us grow up to fit into it.

"But you are a chosen generation, a royal priesthood, a holy nation,
His own special people, that you may proclaim the praises of Him who
called you out of darkness into His marvelous light;"

— 1 Peter 2:9, NKJV

Royalty can be defined as people of royal blood or status.
Because God has adopted us as His own we are grafted in as
royalty. We are chosen, His own special people, and we have
the honor to praise Him with our influence in this world. As
we speak and live our lives in God's Word, we are constantly
growing in God's love and increasing more and more until
that love overflows. This overflow will bring a rich revelation
of spiritual insight in all things. We will come to know God
fully as He imparts to us the deepest understanding of all He
does.

We were once like my pretend play. We were attacked by the
greatest deceiver of them all (Satan), and the handsome
King/Prince (Jesus) had to save us all. He did it all. He did the
work and will complete the work in us. I pray just as Paul
prayed,

"I pray with great faith for you because I'm fully convinced that the
One who began this glorious expression of grace in you will faithfully
continue the process of maturing you through your union with him and
will complete it at the unveiling of our Lord Jesus Christ!"

— Philippians 1:6, TPT

It is time to walk and live your life like royalty. You have a
destiny, and it is to be like Christ. Are you living as royalty? Do
you walk daily as the chosen daughter of the King? You have
the influence of a holy nation. It is time for women to rise up
and let Christ's power change our lives and the lives around

us. It is important to be joyful as He transforms us from glory to glory to become like Him.

We have a heavenly calling. It is time for us to love God and others more deeply and more passionately. You have a ministry. It is time to call it forth and move towards this royal calling. Rise up, Royal Woman of Influence.

Prayer:

I pray for a rich revelation of who you called me to be. I pray to know You fully, to understand the deep mysteries of Your ways. I pray we choose the most excellent way and become pure without offense, filled with Your righteousness. Thank You for completing the work You have begun in us. We will walk in this royal identity today. In Jesus' Name, we pray. Amen.

Part III
In Closing

A WORD FOR YOU

The Lord speaks over you:

My desire is to break the mold that restricts you and extend the boundaries in your heart. When you think, "This is the way it will always be. My situation will never change." You must know I will be your surprise light. I will be your hope in the darkness. I will be the strength that stands by you. I will be the revelation light showing the way into My presence. I will be the glory that streams down in the chaos that gives direction, and you will find and feel My presence even in times of trouble and pressure. I will transform your situation with My love. I will ignite a passion so great that your family and those in your path will wonder at the beauty emanating from you. Soak in My love, and rest in these words that I speak to you. The mountains of obstacles before you will melt like wax as I burn you Holy. Stand before Me, and let Me look at your heart, breathing my breath on you like I did to Adam and Eve. One touch from Me will consume your very heart and ignite a passion within you to see Me and My ways more clearly. Get ready for an adventure!

YOUR DAILY DECLARATIONS

Keep these, and recite them daily:

God is good.

God is for me.

I am an influencer.

I am here for such a time as this--the world needs me and what God has put inside of me.

I am known by the King of kings.

I am clean and pure because of Christ's sacrifice on the cross.

I am forgiven, and He calls me: "Flawless One."

I have a sound mind.

I am full of virtue and truth.

I am created in the image of God.

I have been given power and authority to take dominion.

I am a creator--the power of life and death is in my tongue, and I build people up and create and encourage life.

I am the bride of Christ.

I am loved with an everlasting love.

I am a warrior.

I am a combat-booted-bride.

I am God's perfect partner.

I am a daughter of the King.

I am an overcomer.

I am full of God's purpose.

I am God's favorite.

I am powerful.

I rule my feelings.

I am His darling.

I am a love letter.

I am an original.

I am perfect because God made me, and God does not make mistakes.

I am a holy vessel.

I have a Helper in the Holy Spirit.

I can change my perspective.

I have a destiny. There is a plan and purpose for my life.

I fit into the right shoe.

I am not forgotten.

I am not alone. Jesus will never leave nor forsake me.

I am wanted.

I am enough.

I am valuable.

I can move mountains.

I have authority to speak into situations and change them.

I have what it takes.

I am a gift.

I am the theme of God's song.

I was created to arise.

I can repent.

I have a merciful Father God who has forgiven all my sins--past, present, and future.

I have a Restorer.

I am free.

I am a message.

I am His ambassador.

I can write my own epic story with God, and no matter what happened yesterday, today is a new day to write something new.

I am royalty.

The King of kings has called me by name and made me to be a Woman of Influence.

APPENDIX A

Bible Versions Used

Scripture references throughout this devotional book are shown in italics and are followed by the specific reference as well as the Bible version, like this:

The Bible versions referenced in this book are listed here with the abbreviations used.

AMPC Amplified Bible, Classic Edition

KJV King James Version

NASB New American Standard Bible, 1995

NASB, 1977 New American Standard Bible, 1977

NIV New International Version

NKJV New King James Version

NLT New Living Translation

TPT The Passion Translation

ABOUT THE AUTHORS

Katie Walker

Katie Walker is an actress, producer, author, and public speaker with a heart to empower men and women to walk in their purpose. Katie was the supporting lead in the powerful feature film *8 DAYS*. The film has been shown in over 56 countries around the world, bringing awareness to the crime of child sex trafficking in the United States. She has partnered with the nonprofit Sharetogether.org and the film company After Eden Pictures to produce a brand new docuseries to continue fighting this evil crime. Katie recently completed the feature film, *Because of Gracia*, which premiered nationally and internationally on TBN, and produced the short film, *My Father's Son*, by Los Angeles director, Kyle Clements. She starred in a dark comedy *R.I.P.*, directed by Hannah Dorsett, which is currently touring the film festival circuit. She is also actively writing an upcoming TV series with Philipa Booyens about repentance and atonement. She travels around the nation and is co-host with Jennifer Lucky on the international TV show, *Rise Up with Jenny and Katie*, encouraging others to know and accept Jesus Christ as Lord and Savior. Katie is also a teacher for The Passion Translation online Bible study. Katie uses her social platform to share daily devotionals. She lives in Shreveport, LA, with her husband, Todd Walker, and their four children.

Connect with Katie:

twitter.com/katieb_walker

facebook.com/katiewalker

instagram.com/katieb_walker

Philipa A. Booyens

As the Creative Vice President of After Eden Pictures (afteredenpictures.com), Philipa grew up modeling, acting, and working at her family agency in Franklin, Tennessee. An All-American in track and field, this cover girl was also a Jr. Olympic record holder, gold medalist, and a collegiate scholarship athlete before becoming a published author and co-writing the Dove Award nominated feature film, *I'm Not Ashamed*. Philipa is also the screenwriter of the feature film *8 DAYS*, which was made to fight human trafficking in the USA and has been featured on numerous radio and television shows, and has supported over 70 anti-trafficking organizations. Philipa is a sought after speaker for schools, churches, and events and has a passion to transform culture for God's Kingdom through stories that inspire and commission people to be who God called them to be.

Connect with Philipa:

twitter.com/philipabooyens

facebook.com/philipa.booyens

instagram.com/philipabooyens

Women of Influence, it is time to rise up into who God called you to be. Join Katie and Philipa on Mondays and Thursdays at 10am CST for live videos to encourage and challenge you to discover the power and purpose of who you are and to fall more in love with our King Jesus. Connect with us at www.katieandphilipa.com to learn more.

twitter.com/katieandphilipa

facebook.com/katieandphilipa

instagram.com/katieandphilipa

www.katieandphilipa.com

NOTES

Introduction

1. See Esther 4:14b.

1. Women Are Influencers

1. Plutarch's Lives: Life of Mark Antony by Plutarch (XXVII.2-3). Publisher CreateSpace Independent Publishing Platform 12/8/2015.
2. Parks, Rosa; James Haskins (1992). Rosa Parks: My Story. Dial Books p. 116.
3. See John 4:5-29.
4. Saints and Sisterhood: The Lives of Forty-eight Holy Women by Eva Catafygiotu Light and Life Publishing Company
5. Ibid.

3. Your Identity

1. See Genesis 12:1-4.
2. See Genesis 21:1-3.
3. See Mark 8:33.
4. See Luke 22:54-65.
5. See Leviticus 19:29.
6. See Deuteronomy 22:21.
7. See Joshua 6:23.
8. SeeMatthew 1:5.
9. See Joshua 2:2-7 and 15-22.
10. https://www.biblegateway.com/resources/all-women-bible/rahab
11. See Romans 8:17a and Colossians 2:10, NIV.
12. See Hebrews 11:6.
13. See Genesis 1:26.
14. See Genesis 1.
15. See John 19:30 along with the TPT footnotes.
16. Brian Simmons, "Song of Solomon Part 1" posted from HealingWatersNY YOUTUBE channel.
17. Ibid.
18. Film Gladiator (2000) spoken by the character Maximus, played by Russell Crowe, directed by Ridley Scott.

Day 1—You Are God's Favorite

1. See Song of Solomon 1:8, TPT.
2. See Song of Solomon 6:9, TPT.

Day 2—You Are Powerful

1. See 1 John 4:8.
2. See 1 John 4:18.

Day 3—You Rule Your Feelings

1. Meyer, Joyce. Battlefield of the Mind: How to win the war in your mind. Tulsa, OK Harrison House, 1995.

Day 4—You Are His Darling

1. See Song of Songs 4:1-5.

Day 5—You Are a Love Letter

1. Pastor DawnChere Wilkerson: Lost Letter sermon from YouTube Shreveport Community Church 11/26/2017.

Day 8—You Are a Holy Vessel

1. See Colossians 3:16, NKJV.
2. See Psalm 139:23.

Day 12—You Fit Into the Right Shoe

1. See Colossians 1:16 and Hebrews 12:2.
2. See Jeremiah 29:11.

Day 23—You Can Repent

1. See 2 Chronicles 7:14.

Day 25—You Have A Restorer

1. Isaiah 11:11a footnote from The Passion Translation
2. Isaiah 11:11b footnote from The Passion Translation
3. Isaiah 11:11c footnote from The Passion Translation
4. Isaiah 11:11d footnote from The Passion Translation
5. Isaiah 11:11e footnote from The Passion Translation